URSULA or UNIVERSITY

URSULA or UNIVERSITY

STEPHANIE YOUNG

KRUPSKAYA • 2013

ACKNOWLEDGMENTS

Many books informed this one; most are named within. I am particularly indebted to *American Babylon* by Robert O. Self and *No There There* by Chris Rhomberg for Oakland history.

Thanks to all the friends and loved ones past and present whose conversation and presence have so profoundly shaped this work. It wouldn't exist without the generosity of those who read drafts and responded along the way: Del Ray Cross, Jess Heaney, Robin Lasser, Lauren Levin, Tom Marshall, Ron Palmer, Nancy Popp, Yosefa Raz, Camille Roy (and everyone in the Fall 2011 workshop), Amy Trachtenberg, Cynthia Sailers, Juliana Spahr, Dana Ward, and Alli Warren. I'm grateful to the artist residency program at Montalvo Arts Center for time and space, to the editors at *Jacket2* and *The Poetry Project Newsletter* where some of this writing first appeared, and to Kevin Killian and Jocelyn Saidenberg for publishing books that have meant so much to me over the years. For bringing this one into the world, among them. To Clive for everything.

Copyright © Stephanie Young
Book Design: Wayne Smith
Distibuted by Small Press Distribution, Berkeley, CA
www.spdbooks.org

ISBN 978-1-928650-35-5

KRUPSKAYA
306 Rutledge Street
San Francisco, CA 94110
www.krupskayabooks.com

Essay (after Bernadette Mayer). 9

January 2011. 15

REPOPORT. 33

Mutual Aid. 63

Black Swan. 77

The Golden Handcuffs. 81

Post Camp Messianism. 85

Bay of Angels 95

In which metaphors for poetry
communties, and for writing
about them, abound 113

The Fast 123

Summer 2011 129

The Wind Blows 151

ESSAY
after Bernadette Mayer

I guess it's too late to live on the farm

I guess it's too late to enter the darkened room in which a single light illuminated the artist stripped from the waist down, smeared with blood, stretched and bound to the table

I guess it's too late to inhabit a glass-fronted, white, box-like room, dressed in white, against which the menstrual blood was visible

I guess it's too late to start farming

I guess it's too late to start struggling to remain standing in a transparent plastic cubicle filled with wet clay, repeatedly slipping and falling

I guess it's too late to buy 60,000 acres in Marfa

I guess it's too late to begin appearing on the subway in stinking clothes during rush hour with balloons attached to her ears, nose, hair and teeth

I guess we'll never have an orgiastic Happening

I guess we're too old to carry out maintenance activities in public spaces, during public hours

I guess we couldn't afford to simulate masturbation while President Josip Broz Tito's motorcade drove by below

I guess we're not suited to "I am awake in the place where women die"

I guess we'll never have a self-inflicted wound in front of an audience now

I guess entering a sex cinema dressed in a black shirt, jeans with the crotch removed, and a machine gun slung over her shoulder is not in the cards now

I guess Clive wouldn't make a good photographic montage in which their male and female faces became almost indistinguishable

I guess I can't expect we'll ever have a selection of photographs derived from images produced by the beauty industry now

I guess I'll have to give up all my dreams of being seen, clothed and unclothed, being systematically measured by two male 'researchers' who record her measurements on a chart and compare them with a set of 'normal' measurements

I guess I'll never be waiting for my body to break down, to get ugly

We couldn't get tied together by our hair anyways though Allen Ginsberg got one late in life

Maybe someday I'll have the foreshortened barrel of a gun pointing toward the viewer

I guess joining our hands around the base's perimeter fence into which they weave strands of wool is really out

Feeding the pigs and the chickens, walking between miles of rows of crops

I guess examining women's working conditions is just too difficult

We'll never have a, never-really-a-collective, a group of women who came together to work on a public mural

Too much work and still to be poets

Who are the simultaneously-the-beneficiary-of-our-cultural-heritage-and-a-victim-of-it-poets

Was there ever a poet who had a self-sufficient loss of certainty

Flannery O'Connor raised peacocks

And Wendell Berry has raised large-scale spirals of rusted industrial materials in incongruous natural and commercial spaces

Faulkner may have spent three days in a gallery with a coyote, a little

And Robert Frost asked a friend to shoot him at close range with a .22 caliber rifle

And someone told me Samuel Beckett lay hidden under a gallery-wide ramp, masturbating while vocalizing into a loudspeaker his fantasies about the visitors walking above him

Very few poets are really going to the library carrying a concealed tape recording of loud belches

If William Carlos Williams could be a doctor and Charlie Vermont too, If Yves Klein could be an artist, and Jackson Pollock too,

Why not a poet who was also dying of lymphoma and making a series of life size photographs, self-portrait watercolors, medical object-sculptures and collages made with the hair she lost during chemotherapy

Of course there was Brook Farm
And Virgil raised bees
Perhaps some poets of the past were overseers of the meticulous
chronicle of the feeding and
        excretory cycles of her son during the first six months of his life
I guess poets tend to live more momentarily
Than life in her body as the object of her own sculpting activity would allow
You could never leave the structures made of wood, rope and concrete
blocks assembled to form
        stocks and racks, to give a reading
Or to go to a lecture by Emerson in Concord
I don't want to be continuously scrubbing the flesh off of cow bones
with a cleaning brush but
        my mother was right
I should never have tried to rise out of the proletariat
Unless I can convince myself as Satan argues with Eve
That we are among a proletariat of poets of all the classes
Each ill-paid and surviving on nothing
Or on as little as one needs to survive
Steadfast as any person's glottis, photographed with a laryngoscope,
speaking the following
        words: "The power of language continues to show its trace for
a long time after silence"
        and fixed as the stars
Tenants of a vision we rent out endlessly

JANUARY 2011

I have to begin with this failure. This thing I made that failed. I should maybe be more seductive about it. Like Eileen Myles' *Inferno*, that first line: "My English professor's ass was so beautiful." When she read at the college where I work, Eileen said prose always begins for her with one line. Once she had "My English professor's ass was so beautiful" she knew she could write everything else she needed to. Had to. Eileen is one of the vocational poets. The idea of vocation was lately a lot in the air, one of the ideas in the air around the poets I hang around with. As I write this, vocation is in the air, somewhere to the side, a space I can't quite squeeze myself into. *Inferno* is a book about becoming a poet, some of the social stuff around becoming a poet, the institutional stuff around becoming a poet. I'm trying to write something about being a poet in the middle of feeling confused about the social stuff, the institutional stuff.

I feel a little squeamish about Eileen's line, maybe because I'm somebody's English professor. Maybe Eileen could only publish *Inferno* with its first line about a beautiful ass after she no longer worked at UCSD. But these are the strands for later: the university, the teacher, the poets I hang around with, what you can and can't publish if you want to be an English professor, is that even true, the awkwardness of being a kind of insubstantial English professor and hyper-competent academic administrator, always afraid of losing my job, of losing it, a poet who hangs around mostly with other poets who are more or less substantial English professors, programmers, program directors, coordinators, booksellers, psychoanalytic psychotherapists, literacy advocates, graduate students, parents, fundraisers for non profits, ghostwriters for fundraisers, administrators of all kinds, unemployed, executive assistants, salespeople for drug companies, receptionists, also

Michael Gottlieb's *The Jobs of the Poets*, all the ideas in the air, how they evaporate or condense or something like salt on your skin after you've stopped sweating, but also sometimes a rash. Stuff like that.

The thing I made that failed is a movietelling, or neo-benshi, piece. I was invited to make it for a group show that never happened. Jeanne/Joan: a few of us would make pieces using films featuring Jeanne Moreau, and then Mac McGinnes and Cedar Sigo were collaborating on one longer piece organized around Joan Crawford, Mac stitching together this symphonic bio-pic using scenes from every film she'd ever done. I was inspired. The thing I made that failed used scenes from four different films. It's 26 minutes long, with 7 sections, over-ambitious and over-edited. Sometimes two different scenes play side by side, so that it's difficult to know what to watch. I wrote it fast, in January 2009, in order to perform what I thought would be the first draft at a Segue reading the next month. My previous movietelling pieces were all short, under ten minutes, always working with a single scene, mostly associative and never doing that thing which can make these performances so knee-jerkingly pleasurable to watch, that lipsynching thing where you can put words into an actor's mouth that they never said but which look about right, so that in her version of *Rebel Without a Cause*, Roxi Hamilton can make James Dean say "I don't need a Daddy in a dress, five of the most famous men in Hollywood have sucked my cock." I wanted to finally try the lipsynching thing, which had always been beyond me, and I did manage to pull it off for about 3 minutes in the first section. But I was writing so quickly, and so much was going on, was on my mind, that I slipped into doing what I always do—the thing I made that failed was mostly associative, with fragmented lines, language taken from newspapers and government reports. I think the thing I made that failed was partly about wishing I was a filmmaker, the way Warren Sonbert talks about it. I tried to put a lot of shots into relation. I wanted to respond to ideas and events as they arrived, were arriving.

I wanted there to be room for everything, and also I wanted to say something. Some tension between these desires.

I tried to weave together a lot of strands in the thing I made that failed. Dodie Bellamy says "How to establish the threads that I want to weave can be maddening." And it was. I probably established too many. I could have just let Moreau be the strands. That would have been enough. Moreau plus one other thing, something easy like poets at parties, something I was definitely thinking a lot about at the time I made the thing that failed. But also Oscar Grant. How BART is a public transportation system designed to serve some people and not others. Designed to move certain workers at certain times between certain neighborhoods. How money moves around. How information moves around. The internet. Gossip. Carriers of all kinds—how one poet's work will appear in another, but not just work, and not just poets, how all sorts of a person will appear in another, persons will appear in persons. All their neuroses, education, weapons, thoughtfulness, love, saliva, fear, money, guilt, pin #, language, forms and records, sweat and envy. All their energy. Vibes. History. Feast days, reversals, uncanny knowledge. The dead. My father among them. Fear of earthquakes, fear especially of being in the BART transbay tube during an earthquake, during a big one. The Hayward Fault.

Chris Kraus says "Anne Rower says when you're writing in real time you have to revise a lot. By this I think she means that every time you try and write the truth it changes. More happens. Information constantly expands." And she said that in 1996. What's real time?

I'm reading *I Love Dick* again, and Ariana Reines on tumblr, the feeling I get from this my reading helps me know how I failed, I'm failing but I can't seem to stop. Ariana says "Rumor and information are often inseparable in Haiti." And "I used to think that there was nothing I couldn't tell but it isn't true." And "my mother's father died on the millennium. His death hid her homelessness and my brother's suffering, which would come after." And "I've written that Haitians refer to the earthquake of January 12, 2010 as 'the event.' It seems to me one event may hide another, as in the poem by Kenneth Koch."

This thing I made that failed moved along a similar impulse, stringing events together like trains. Sliding one past another, snagging unrelated things. Like Chris Kraus, "I'm sensing that the farthest point of synchronicity is fear and dread." What's an event. Ariana's post, New Year's Revolution, begins with "An environment of secrecy." This keeps rubbing against Anne Boyer's status update, YEAR OF CANDOR. Rubbing up inside me.

I'm beginning to understand that the thing I made that failed did so for a central reason, and the reason was a sound nobody recognized, and the failure is because of where I placed it, a kind of epigraph, at the beginning, in a loop, in the dark. It's the first thing you hear, the roar of the crowd in the early hours of New Years Day 2009, half in, half out of the train, stopped at the Fruitvale BART station, captured on somebody's cell phone, later posted to YouTube, but the thing I made that failed didn't say any of that, it was just a sound, like air being sucked out of the room, or a long collective drawn out NO, moan of the wind outside a house during a blizzard, on the prairie, pandemonium, the sounds that came before, and the sounds that came after the shot that killed Oscar Grant, shot in the back by BART cop Johannes Mehserle at close range, Grant is on the ground, on his stomach, he's unarmed, but you can't see that in the thing I made that failed, it's only sound, of the shot itself, and the brief but total silence surrounding the shot, the sound has so many parts, there's a low wail running through it, holding it together.

In the early hours of New Years Day 2009 I was with my friends the poets at a party in Berkeley. Some people were leaving one party for another, or going home, or cleaning up. Driving down the hill.

Somewhere in the middle of the thing I made that failed, I quoted Bataille, I was trying to say something about Oscar Grant's murder as unexceptional, as symptomatic, as the Reverend Lynice Pinkard says, "Let's be clear: The shooting of Oscar Grant in the back by BART police officer Johannes Mehserle was horrific, but it was not 'crazy.' It was not the act of a rogue cop or even a 'poorly trained' one. In reality, the forces of unbridled self-interest and private ownership, interlinked with and supported by white supremacy, have so shaped what it means to be a police officer that Johannes Mehserle was doing little more than what he was set up to do."

Bataille says "In the upside down world of feast-days the orgy occurs at the instant when the truth of that world reveals its overwhelming force."

In the upside down world of a holiday, BART runs all night. The murder of an unarmed African American man occurs when the truth of that world reveals its overwhelming force. In the upside down world of a holiday, the mostly white poets I am and hang out with are across town, in a beautiful house that's difficult to reach by public transportation. None of us own the house, but we do have access because three of us have worked there at different times. One of us lives there now. The owner is out of town. We play music, and talk and laugh and love each other, we eat rich expensive foods and drink delicious wine and spirits and some of the poets make out in pairs and groups, and this is also unexceptional. We were doing little more than we were set up to do. The mostly white poets I am and hang out with learned about the murder of the African American man on the internet the next day. Perhaps a handful of the mostly white poets I am and hang out with may have attended the January 7, 2009 march in protest of this murder. I'm not sure. There's no reason I couldn't have been at the march. It's not like I didn't know it was happening. I saw announcements all over the internet. But I wasn't.

One section from the thing I made that failed is sort of about that march. The scene is from *Diary of a Chambermaid*. Moreau stands on a ladder, leaning over a stone wall to gossip with the farmer next door and the woman who is both his servant and lover. The farmer's servant-lover stutters, because I was trying to fit the words into her mouth, which wasn't working out very well, she says "It wasn't a riot until / The associated press // it wasn't a riot until," cut to a shot of the farmer's indignant face, "They destroyed police property!" Earlier in this scene Moreau, the farmer, and his servant-lover have carried on a confused conversation about BART, how the trains are carpeted and that's gross, how it doesn't run after midnight, isn't designed finally for needs beyond those of the market. Other victims of the BART police force, all African American men. Jerrold Hall, 1992. Bruce Seward, 2001. During this conversation, Moreau, the farmer, and his servant-lover also comment briefly on the plot of the movie they're appearing in. The farmer, who at this point in the scene is myself, says to Moreau, who is also, at this point, myself, "it could be you're worried about the wrong things." All my neuroses and phobia of riding BART, of being in the tube during an earthquake, and the tube cracking, and flooding, and dying down there.

Abigail Child introduced herself after I performed the thing I made that failed at the Segue series in New York on February 14, 2009. Dodie's birthday. Steve Benson also performed that day, he was marvelous and sweet and smart and wove pieces from our conversation into his performance, conversation from a half hour before, walking down the street after lunch. Songlines. He did it on the spot. Wove in so many things from so many conversations with so many different people in the audience. You could hear it in the room, what he was doing bounced back, bounced around. He wove the room together, a humidifier of ideas and relations in the air.

Abigail asked afterwards where's the S/M scene from? I couldn't remember. I didn't understand. I hadn't thought of it, any of it, as

S/M, although I did bring up Sade, it wasn't a sex scene. Abigail meant, I realized, the scene from *Touchez pas au Grisbi*, where Jean Gabin slaps everybody in the room—Moreau, Dora Doll, the porter. Gabin slaps the porter with the man's own wallet.

I couldn't remember the name of this movie when she asked me. Couldn't remember the name of the movie from a piece I'd performed only moments before. *Something something Grisbi*, I said. Abigail was not impressed.

I read some lines about poetry communities and the internet while this scene from *Touchez pas au Grisbi* played. The scene was slowed down. Not way down, but down. I'd like to put a picture here. *Touchez pas au Grisbi* was Moreau's first film. She's very young in it. Compared to *Jules et Jim*. Alan Bernheimer told me about *Touchez pas au Grisbi* when I mentioned my Jeanne Moreau constraint project at a dinner party. I rushed to Netflix the next day. In a story about friendship between men, Moreau and Dora Doll are leaky mistresses. Earlier, Dora Doll has appeared dressed like a gigantic baby. That's her job as a showgirl. To dress as a gigantic baby, and carry a gigantic bottle. Dora Doll is with Gabin's friend, the less smart gangster. She leaks his information and Gabin catches her at the club, in the act, with a rival. Throws her against the wall of her dressing room. Really he's mad at his less intelligent friend, for trusting a big leaky baby. This is why Moreau and Dora Doll are hiding in a hotel. They leaked, and now they're in trouble.

The sound is off, and I'm sitting at a table to the side of the room talking into a microphone, it seemed important not to stand on stage, to be with everyone while I spoke, like a sound effect coming from within the group, sometimes what I say hooks up briefly with Gabin's mouth, he's shouting at Moreau, it looks like he's saying "feeeeeelings," while Moreau, backed against the door, points away from herself, I breathlessly repeat, "took a photo … put it on the internet," the only sound other than my voice is a loop of Gabin slamming the door of the hotel room, slapping people. The loop is muffled, voices or whispers, speech peeled away from its narrative drive, stretched out, the door when it slams sounds like a groan from a far room. The slaps sound like the crack of a gunshot. It seems to me that one sound may hide another. The sounds are sort of gothic. And S/M.

In retrospect, the lines I read during this scene seem flimsy, in that they only made some small comment on the spectacular forms of sociability that had so recently taken over my life. Blogs, flickr, myspace, facebook. My poetry community autobiography went something like that, with the Buffalo poetics listserv of the 90s as a kind of epigraph in which I watched but didn't speak. It was terribly exciting at first, to become participation, and then it wavered and felt bad. On the subject of these bad feelings I am mute or stupid. I narrate them to myself, obsessive thought without much understanding, with a longing for something like structural critique. A critique of the networks and systems that surround and produce poetry communities, a critique arising, or moving away from, that at least doesn't leave out my feelings. Maybe that's impossible. I often tell myself the bad feelings are just part of it, of the good feelings too, of being with a group, hanging out with poets, for long enough now to say with some assurance probably for the rest of my life. Individual feelings, triggered by individual relationships. What group? But sometimes an idea that some networked platforms where I met and meet my friends, the poets, some login pages, some linking strategies, might have something to do with the bad feelings. The peculiar, magnifying effect of a larger than local network on the local. That's one thing.

And then something about the house, how the readings, what felt like the most exciting readings, and the friendliest, increasingly moved into private, into the semi-private house, at the time I was becoming participation. My living room, too. How the reading went from being terrifyingly public to terrifyingly private, but documented in a kind of semi-public of the internet. Some found the living room readings more accessible. Warmer. Others found them less so, from the second floor entrance and no elevator to the limits of anyone's invite list. You couldn't just put your address on the internet. Could you?

In the archive of my enthusiasms, a manic attention to everyone, I am in love with the room, becoming participation on the networked platform means becoming participation in the room with others. The local living room. There's this moment when my enthusiasm fails me, but I can't place it. Or maybe I fail it, maybe I wasn't ever meant to become participation, although I could float in on girlish enthusiasm, I enjoyed my body's sex, the performance of its assigned gender, it's fun when you're young, but the culture finds girlish enthusiasm distasteful in aging women and I received this message well, so well I never knew, but did secrete the message through my glands. Maybe I gave myself the rash.

Kathy Acker says "The old actress isn't good anymore. But she keeps on acting even though she knows all the audiences mock her hideousness and lack of context cause she adores acting. Her legs are grotesque: FLABBY."

At the reading in New York with Steve Benson where I first performed the thing that failed, with its many tangled parts, many tangled images, I was sort of received as yet another Bay Area poet obsessed with the gossip of a Bay Area poetry community, with a myopic Bay Area feeling around me. I was perhaps easy to dismiss on these terms. But also, many of the mostly white poets I am and hang out with in New York were at the annual conference of the Association of Writers & Writing Programs that weekend. A conference mostly for and about MFA in creative writing programs in the U.S., of which there were 15 in 1975 and 184 in 2010, a fact of astonishing growth which the AWP seems proud of and even takes some credit for, this fact of murky contention and debate in many poetry communities. And yet no matter how ambivalent you might feel about the AWP, or the boom in MFA creative writing programs, or the professionalization of a community art form, or the impact this structural change has had on literary cultural production in the U.S., if you are a small press publisher of poetry it's become increasingly important to have a table at the AWP conference book fair, because so many of the writers and readers of contemporary poetry are or will be connected to an MFA program in creative writing at one time or another. Thus, in February 2009, when I first performed the thing I made that failed in New York, when many of the mostly white poets I am and hang out with in New York were at AWP, I didn't know that many people in the room, or I knew them only by name. The room was full of important people of an older generation, many of whom came of age as poets in the Bay Area, before the astonishing growth in MFA in creative writing programs.

I am trying to narrate the failure of this thing from the future in such a way that takes into account something I cannot see, something about a place somewhat obsessed with itself, its sexual relations, utopian drives, reading groups, living rooms, epic talking, fashion, institutions, petty grievances, omissions, after parties, breakups. I felt bad, I feel pretty bad. I don't know if it is only individual. It seems sometimes to get worse, then a little better, then a little worse.

As I am trying to narrate the failure of this thing from the future in such a way that takes into account something I cannot see, I read this piece to Del, sitting in his living room, eating Thai food, drinking wine. We've been doing something like this for 10 years. We eat carbs and read our writing to each other, and others along the way. Ron Palmer right now but he couldn't make it that night. Tim, Cassie, Jennifer, Yuri. Susannah. Kate, Taylor, Cynthia, Catherine. 10 years.

It's a long time. It'll get longer. Del says *oh it's good it's very funny, very hyperbolic, you know you're being hyperbolic, right?* He means about the failure, that it only makes sense as hyperbole, says *come on, there's no way you can know if the thing failed or not*. At the end of the night, the truest thing, he hopes I don't really think I'm a failure. Because he cares about me. We talk about the way Del feels more on the edge of the poetry social scene I feel incredibly invested in, sometimes desperately so. But it's not like Del is checked out, it's the 10-year anniversary of *Shampoo*, he reads everybody.

I feel a little hot in the face, I'm not sure I knew I was being hyperbolic, was I being hyperbolic? I did think the thing I made failed, as I am writing this, feel that way for sure, but the more I think about it the more confused I become regarding the terms of this failure. I wrote this paragraph before I realized the failure of the sound nobody recognized. But it's also true that I often don't know what I'm doing, or trying to do, when I begin. It's difficult to say if I went for A, and B happened instead, or what. I become slowly convinced on the drive back from Del's that a central dimension of my failure was social.

I'm thinking this partly through reading Renee Gladman's *To After That (Toaf)* which could be described as a book about a failed novella, but that would be only half right. It's a book writing through the problems of a novella that wasn't in the world, not really, until it became *To After That (Toaf)*. The novella that failed did live in a few individual hands other than Renee's along the way, as drafts. It even moved one reader to come. That seems the opposite of failure.

I'm feeling envious of Renee Gladman's writing, envious and alienated by its distance, its skepticism: "It is amazing the things we think have affected us, especially in retrospect." A coolness towards the city in which the failed novella began, a city of great attachments and meaning in the book, "the area," the Bay Area. The writing is cool at the hottest points, she names no names, or names them Chubby. Her lover at the time, S. "On January 28, 2000 I attended a reading at a popular local venue for experimentation. (I am still combing my journals for corroboration: I did write this book: I did try hard to write it.) I do not know whose reading it was, but in those days, I was in the habit of taking notes. This event was held in the city, where 'the problem of the person'—my problem—was made evident."

My problem, too. The problem of the person. I think she means Small Press Traffic. The popular venue for experimentation. I would always say Small Press Traffic. If it was me, writing that. Or I would say SPT. And think later how I'd once again written something that meant something particular to a small group of people in a local. A local room.

In the thing I made that failed there's this slightly hysterical mode of naming names, conversations, influences. Especially in one section, I think I look a little desperate in it. But I wanted to make so many others visible and audible in the room, wanted to drag up every pressure or gift or fortuitous encounter that helped me think, or hurt, or pushed me over edges into other edges. This winds up being the place where gossip comes in, I describe a reading by Erika Staiti in which she "*talked about some problems she loves in the relations among poets and how long it takes the poets to accept a non-poet, like a year, which the non-poet earns basically by showing up and being persistent, and how nobody ever brings non-poets around because the poets ignore them. She also talked about the poets making out with each other in various combinations and groups, ways the making out in groups gets talked about and how even if you haven't made out you've participated in the way you've chosen to talk about the making out or not.*" I also talked about the purple notebook Julian gave me, he found it when we were helping Cynthia move, his old purple notebook, DREAMS on the cover in black sharpie, and I wrote the drafts for the thing I made that failed inside this notebook. Gossip like that. In New York and then again when I performed the thing that failed a second and last time in Cincinnati, I had to rush during this section, in order to get it all out, or get it all in, during the scene I'd cut to go alongside. It's from *The Lovers,* and loops several times inside the thing I made that failed. Sometimes I placed it side by side with the scene from *Diary of a Chambermaid,* I kept placing these scenes together because the house in which Jeanne Moreau is a bourgeois wife looks remarkably similar to the one in which she is a chambermaid. In this scene from the *The Lovers,* she wears a long white dressing gown, and leaves her husband and children sleeping in the house to wander through a hedge, young lover at her side, or sometimes just behind. She rests her head against a wooden post, they gaze into the night sky. She runs towards a clump of trees and he pursues her. In the morning they run away in his car. She realizes she's made a mistake.

Clive was with me when I performed the thing that failed in New York, and he loved me when he said afterwards *you really love your friends.* The one thing Del really objected to in this piece so far was the moment when I describe myself as perhaps easy to dismiss as yet another Bay Area poet obsessed with the Bay Area. Del thought I should not be apologetic about coterie, or friendship, whatever you want to call it. Del called it coterie.

But the thing I made that failed maybe obscured some ambivalence. Or some tension, feelings that are the opposite of love but also love. I didn't know how to write these things. Maybe the thing I made that failed had a critique about poetry communities. Maybe this is part of what I mean about being perhaps easy to dismiss as yet another Bay Area poet, because the thing I made that failed could be read as a tube of gossip from one side of the continent to the other, a tube that seemed to amplify or even valorize that gossip, and if you were in the audience I could imagine thinking why are we supposed to care? The gossip wasn't even new at that point, was pointedly a little old, and stale, as gossip tends to go as a commodity. I think I might have been trying to say something about gossip as an event that hides other events. And the thing I made that failed wound up doing this exactly. The gossip came through the tube loud and clear, the group, but not much else. And yet, neither did I want to disavow gossip as epistemology, productive of meaning, of groups, a creek or stream running under the development, alongside its idealization, getting everything all wet.

The weird thing is that I never even performed the thing that failed in the Bay Area.

When you're writing in real time you have to revise a lot. On June 19, 2009, Johannes Mehserle pleaded not guilty to charges of murder and the jury trial was scheduled to begin in October. Mehserle's attorney Michael Rains sought a change of venue of the trial on the grounds that there would not be an impartial jury in Alameda County. Citing extensive media coverage and social upheaval, the judge agreed. Rains' request was honored on October 16, and downtown Los Angeles was chosen on November 19. The trial began on June 10, 2010. On July 8, Mehserle was found guilty of involuntary manslaughter and not guilty of second degree murder and voluntary manslaughter. Nearly 80 people were eventually arrested in protests following the verdict.

Extensive media coverage and social upheaval. A lot has been said about the cell phone video that captured the roar of the crowd in the early hours of New Years Day 2009, half in, half out of the train, stopped at the Fruitvale BART station, the video later posted to YouTube, its impact on bringing Mehserle to trial. And yet the capitalist system of which I am part, recipient of its benefits, resources and power, of separate and unequal justic, still obtained. The cell phone video shows something unexceptional. Something that could not be changed or transformed inside a U.S. courtroom.

I still don't know why I put these things together in the thing I made that failed, why I am doing it right now, trying to write about the mostly white poets I am and hang out with, desire and bad feelings, alongside the sound of the shot that killed Oscar Grant. Snagged on this problem. I read this piece to Clive a few nights ago and he said he still doesn't see the connection. It would be a big mistake if this piece seems to be discussing the system-sponsored murder of an African American man by a white BART cop as metaphor for something about poetry community. Maybe it's more like, something is happening in the same place where the mostly white poets I am and hang out with are thinking a lot about radical history and social movements, yet I seem not to be writing a poem about something that's happening that has a lot to do with those concerns. I keep commenting on the plot of the movie I'm in. Is the piece *about* self-involvement, or is it just self-involved? And shouldn't you be able to tell which it is?

It's the writing about Jennifer Harbury in *I Love Dick* that I'm least sure of. Chris Kraus isn't sure either, "what Guatemalan genocide had to do with the 180 pages of love letters that I'd written with my husband and then given you, like a timebomb or a cesspool or a manuscript. But I would, I would." She's at Dick's house when she writes that. Or experiences that. They're going to have sex for the first and I think only time. "I felt like we were facing each other from the edges of a very dark and scary crater. Truth and difficulty. Truth and sex. I was talking, you were listening. You were witnessing me become this crazy and cerebral girl, the kind of girl that you and your entire generation vilified."

Was that it? I faced you. From the edges of a very dark and scary crater. You was bigger than Dick. I needed you to be bigger than Dick.

When you're writing in real time you have to revise a lot. In June 2010 there was this academic poetics conference in New York. *Rethinking*

Poetics. And then in August 2010 there was this community poetics conference in Oakland. *Labor Day 2010.*

There were similarities and differences between the conferences. Each conference naturalized its vocabulary and value system. Its conflicts and institutions. This naturalization had to do with the way the two conferences were organized, but also how they were received. I had arguments with both. I wrote through my arguments with the first conference in the semi-public of the internet.

I wonder now who it was I had in mind exactly, while writing this report on Rethinking Poetics. I called it REPOPORT. I imagined its possible reader divided, a projection of my own discomfort. How could I speak to others who had attended Rethinking Poetics while at the same time speaking to the mostly white poets I am and hang out with in the Bay Area who had not? Most of my friends in the Bay Area had not. Some had a critique of, had caught feelings around, Rethinking Poetics.

The tone is weird. There are several typos. Some older sense of the internet, the archive, stops me from redacting pieces of this report now. Showing one's work, letting the error stand alongside so much obsessively recounted information. I did little else for a few days. Time was moving on, the conversation would shift any minute, it felt important to join in, in semi-public. Maybe this sense of pressure produced all the repetition, the "so but maybe," the "too too long," the tentative and girlish performance of a self not only thinking aloud, but calling something or someone out, making assertions. In the report I can't stop describing my job, the divided feeling. Apologizing for it. I appear abject, maybe I needed to, which is how I actually felt, feel now, in order to say something. Was it always so? In the archive of my enthusiasms? Is it always the case, in what appears to me now as relentlessly gendered performance, in the semi-public of the internet.

REPOPORT
(posted June 16, 2010, *http://could-be-otherwise.blogspot.com/*)

Eleni Stecopoulos "Never underestimate how much the academy likes to talk about itself." Laughing with the memory of this advice to the young grad student, all the way down B'way after the conference.
Yesterday at 7:55am · Comment · Like

The experience we come to describe as a boring road trip movie about two girls at the academic poetics conference comes to an end on the plane with a manic, sleep-deprived research project: once again we are counting things as a way of thinking about feeling, thinking through confusion, in this case counting degrees earned by panelists at the Rethinking Poetics Conference at Columbia University: BA, MA, Phd, MFA. Also we are tracking the granting institution of these degrees, along with each panelist's current place of employment. We try, for a while, to track connections between panelists and Marjorie Perloff, this diagram includes categories such as "student of," "blurbed by," "has written about Perloff's work," "work has been written about by Perloff," and "connected in some social/institutional way we don't understand," but this proves more difficult to track on the internet.

We've succumbed to purchasing inflight internet service for the purposes of this deranged research, despite our intentions during this boring road trip movie to be the kind of girls who take the subway instead of a cab from and to the airport, a joke we've been joking all weekend, this "we're the kind of girls" joke, which means something like, well first of all we're not girls, but also we are, the kind of girls who are doing this road trip as cheaply as possible because we are the kind of girls who are sharing Juliana's faculty travel funds to pay for this trip, because I'm an admin coordinator + adjunct, thus ineligible for travel funds, and Juliana's travel funds come nowhere close to covering costs for both of us, so we will be the kind of girls who bring granola, and blueberries from Juliana's garden, and eat this for breakfast with yogurt from the bodega, or we will be the kind of girls who get coffee and breakfast sandwiches at starbucks using the starbucks card Clive was given as an end-of-the-semester gift by some kids at the middle school where he is not a teacher but directs the school play which the middle school students pay to participate in, or maybe he was given this card by some kids in the middle school classrooms where he provides arts education funded by an outside non-profit arts organization, because the relatively middle and upper class public schools where he works still have little or no budget for arts education. He gets a lot of food-related gift cards from the kids and their families at these schools. It's possible I will finish writing this too-much-report at pizzaiolo, where I will purchase my coffee and toast with a pizzaiolo gift certificate gifted to him by the same kids, re-gifted to me. So while we are not the kind of girls who pay to watch *Did you hear about the Morgans?* or purchase inflight internet service, we are also the kind of girls who do. Mostly we are the kind of girls who are so, so exhausted.

Juliana looks things up on the internet and I take sprawling, loopy notes on a yellow notepad, later we cannot read these things written in blue ink and keep counting and re-counting. Here, let me look at that. Again, like, uh, other things we have counted, the numbers are both boringly obvious and particularly interesting where they help us notice a category we have naturalized; for instance Juliana notices the preponderance of 1990s Buffalo student, the Charles Bernstein student (herself, Elizabeth Willis, Ben Friedlander, Jena Osman, Jonathan Skinner.)

If you are someone who attended this conference or has been reading about it, you are probably like Stephanie no duh. Me too, but! The particulars! What's been far more at the front of my mind during this road trip is the extreme whiteness and maleness of conference panelists. On Sunday both categories hovered at 100%.

Counting is helping me think. *Of course* almost 100% of the panelists have tenure track jobs in English departments. *Of course* nearly 100% of the panelists with tenure track jobs in English departments have PhDs from Columbia, Buffalo, Cornell, UC Berkeley, the University of Chicago.

I am intensely interested in those panelists who do not have a PhD. Because I'm one of them, yes, but also because many of my friends are one of them. How am I, how are my friends, together, or not, with these others who don't have a PhD (or don't have an MFA, or don't have a BA?) Some of these people without PhDs nonetheless have tenure track jobs in English departments, almost all of them are born before 1960 and hold some other degree, such as a BA from Harvard, or an MA from Georgetown, or an MFA from Cornell (Charles Bernstein, Joan Retallack and C.S. Giscombe, respectively.) If I'm looking at the excel spreadsheet I'm looking at correctly, only one person born after 1960 has no PhD and also holds a tenure track job in an English Department: Joshua Clover, who does have an MFA. The MFA is represented far less in this room, again, if I've counted right, only 7 participants have MFAs, and 2 are currently enrolled in MFA programs at curious points in poetic "careers", one as a conceptual project, partly about nations and borders, partly about the MFA system itself (Rachel Zolf.) In all other cases, those with only MFA, MA or BA degrees, or those with no degree at all, are correspondingly employed outside the university (Rodrigo Toscano, Monica de la Torre, Sherwin Bitsui) or as administrative or adjunct or provisional faculty within it (Lisa Robertson, myself. Arguably I am far more entrenched and inside than most adjuncts, given that the full-time administrative portion of my job both provides the bulk of my salary and institutionalizes my part-time adjunct teaching labor as permanent, or as semi-permanent, for-so-long-as-this-administrative-job-shall-last, which is probably for-so-long-as-the-private-college-I-work-at-shall-last, despite the fact that this additional part-time adjunct teaching labor is not contracted for more than one semester at a time.) And I should say I have an MFA (as do so many of my friends.)

The MFA seems largely reviled at the conference, held up in certain moments as an *outside* of professionalization, and overproduction of degrees into a field with too-few jobs. That this is obviously also true of the PhD is pointed out during the Q&A following the really great "social field of poetry & poetics" panel on Friday. Still, the conference feels invested in valorizing the degree it circulates around. Later, on Saturday, I hear word of complaints that the panel I participated on, poetics & the academy, focused itself too much around the MFA system, when much of what was discussed—the academic reading series, the seminar, the space of the classroom, what's outside the classroom, what the relationship between these things might be—had as much to do with both PhD and undergraduate programs as it did the MFA. Which is to say that none of these things—the creative writing workshop, the academic reading series, etc.—belong exclusively to the MFA system. Many panelists at the academic poetics conference are teachers of both creative writing and literature, and organizers of academic reading series, just not as many in the context of MFA programs. Again, if I am reading the excel spreadsheet correctly.

So but maybe no wonder I feel intensely weird and between. Those here without a PhD are either currently in the process of earning one, its technology running smoothly in their speech, or they are someone who has entered this particular slice of an academic poetic scene by sheer force of thinking and pushing their way in, making a place for their writing and thinking, making an argument, by the fact of their presence, about the thinking that is obviously done outside the academy, or because their poetry has in some way come to be central to the particular slice of an academic poetic scene constructed here.

Whereas I'm kind of like a weird mole, in the blind and burrowing sense of things. I don't have the right degree, I haven't been pushing my way into this particular location, not exactly exactly. Instead I'm here primarily because of friendship and collaboration with Juliana, a friendship and collaboration born primarily of working at the same institution, but also of being part of overlapping bay area poetry scenes and thus a shared social life. Friendship and collaboration are clearly present in the room in many other relationships but mostly obscured by the holding of right degrees, the pushing, the thinking. In the case of Juliana and me, something seems right up at the surface, something about friendship networks, reciprocity, thinking together, needing one another, alliance at the place where we work. I can't tell if our model of being and thinking together is different than others in the room, or if it is embodying and making visible the kinds of relation that the right degree can obscure.

I sort of feel smuggled in. Snuggled in.

I keep using the word "obscure."

I used to talk and think about myself as someone in resistance to various king-making (prestige) systems, as someone who would speak (smuggle, snuggle) her way into being in relation with other poets, and this will sound willfully naïve but someone who spoke her way into being in relation with other poets somewhat by way of the blog, by way of the blog in 2003. But that speaking into being in relation with other poets was largely uninflected by a sense or an understanding of particular slices of an academic poetic scene, how this particular slice constructs itself around particular degrees and programs, and also uninflected by a sense or understanding of many other scenes.

There was and is a lot I didn't understand. But encountering things such as Juliana's reading reports from U of Hawai'i, or Steve Evans' Third Factory notes, on the internet and before I knew either of them, influenced me greatly. At the same time and maybe this will sound stupid, I didn't register or locate these things inside of institutional or university systems. They felt to the side of those things, they felt like things one does for love. I started blogging because Nada Gordon said something like "Where my laydeeez at."

These three things, people, locations seemed related to me, and not through universities.

I guess what I'm finding most confusing is how this particular slice of an academic poetic scene, as constructed by this conference, is both distinct and separate from the communities where all my love and commitments live, and also very much a part of those relations.

And the thing about feeling kind of weird but also glad that I am at this conference via my friendship and collaboration with Juliana, as if she packed me in her suitcase and snuck me in, which both is and is not true, even as a metaphor, has everything to do with how this particular slice of an academic poet scene, as constructed by this conference, is both distinct and separate from the communities where all my love and commitments live, and yet also very much a part of those relations.

In the room of the conference, I feel somehow not either or any. I've gotten myself into a predicament. I know lots of people in this room but primarily through poetry, not this other thing, this academic poetic thing as constructed by this conference. I would be a lot more comfortable if the context was a reading like, at Segue, or the Zinc Bar, although of course it would be willfully naïve to imagine that things like non-academic reading series don't operate in relation with other systems, to imagine that the non-academic-and-yet-also-itself-an-institution reading series isn't in its own way in relation with an academic poetic scene as constructed by this conference. Among the many relations a non-academic-and-yet-also-itself-an-institution reading series might have.

Here, I'm inside, but not in the way others are. I feel outside, but I'm not. It would be easier to participate if I could project myself into the feeling of being one thing or another, one location or another, but I can't.

The feeling of this conundrum expresses itself with some extremity, if mostly interior. But also, I perspire.

Mark Nowak didn't so much rethink poetics as rethought the same thoughts that led him, 15 years ago, to start publishing/editing XCP. **Sunday at 6:37am · Comment · Like**

I'm here, sigh, blog, fart, burp, because I am so so uncomfortable.

I forgot or I don't know how to speak to the people I live with and love in a *here*, while at the same time loving and speaking to the people who were at the conference, some of whom are strangers and some of whom are also in a *here*.

I don't know how to speak to the people I may not know yet, people I don't have an alliance with yet but would like to.

The academic poetics conference I attended did very little to assist with the latter, except in the negative sense of initiating action or desire towards everyone and everything left outside its space.

And then at the same time it is true that I met the terrific Shelagh Patterson, and that she invited me to visit Pittsburgh. Shelagh has an interesting bio:

"Born and raised in Brooklyn, Shelagh Patterson is currently working towards her doctorate degree in English: Critical and Cultural Studies at the University of Pittsburgh. She received her MFA in Creative Writing, Poetry from the City University of New York Hunter College. She is a recipient of the Bronx Writers' Center's Literary Arts Fellowship and Residency and a Cave Canem Fellow. Her poems have appeared in anthologies, newspapers, magazines, journals, experimental theater, and a feature film."

I love the criss-crosses and intersections there, I love that her poems have appeared in newspapers, and that it is important to her to render such appearances visible in her bio, and how disappointing that these sorts of criss-crosses didn't show up very much at the academic poetics conference. (Yep, I know, there are always exceptions.) I am looking forward to reading Shelagh's poetry. I am looking forward to visiting Pittsburgh, whenever I can get there.

Returning to Mark's facebook comment re: *XCP*, Jen Scappettone says it this way, in a comment stream, talking about a particular kind of damage to the art and the discourse, how conversation at the conference constructed/situated itself in particular frameworks, that is "…the prevalence of white European or Anglo-American humanistic frameworks and their governing assumptions surrounding the relevant past, present, and future of language and culture."

I kept saying to myself and others that the curating at such a rethinking poetics conference needed to be so much more ruthless with itself, by which I mean the powers who constructed, those who held the reins, needed to be ruthless with themselves. Maybe it will sound stupid, but numbers obviously continue to count if such a conference could construct itself in such a homogenous way. It seems like homogeneity is a big problem. At the academic poetics conference, sure, but in lots of non-academic poetics contexts, too, and not just in who gets invited to speak/read/participate, or even who feels welcome and invited in, but also who shows up to listen to who.

Also, what Jen talked about during the panel on materials. I can't stop thinking about it and maybe this is the wrong place for its quotation, the wrong place in this mess I'm writing, but it was something like: not so much making the invisible visible, but bruising its channels of invisibility. Location via the bruise, the damage. And how is this in relation with Jena Osman's ideas around echolocation, locating the unseen via speech, via writing, via sound. Or Sherwin Bitsui, on the question of not speaking, the gentle ruthlessness with which he asks this question of his work, what will be evoked if I write this, what should not be written.

Barrett Watten Poetics R Us.
Monday at 1:09pm · Comment · Like

I keep coming back to biodiversity v. monocultures.

Versus corporate farming.

Nada Gordon I just think... you can't rethink poetics...very well... in the same old theatre of power.
Yesterday at 9:11am · Comment · Like

The room had enormous ceilings. They were almost the sky. There were three large windows behind the table where panelists sat at the front of the room, with a view out onto "The Thinker" (the room was in Philosophy Hall). Also some very big trees.

Performers entered through double doors in the middle of things, onto a wide carpeted walkway dividing the room in half. In the front of the room, on either side of the panelist table, was a vertical phalanx of chairs, sort of like jury boxes, box seats. Theater in the round, sort of.

The jury box, box seats, filled mostly with elders, especially during the first half of the first day, during inauguration of the proceedings. The back half of the room, mostly graduate students and bad kids, too. Signs on the wall in the back said: "when you procrastinate, others are watching" and "your dissertation is waiting." These signs were stressing out some of the graduate students. The room seemed to be otherwise used as a rec room/lounge/dissertation boot camp.

There were maybe 100 people in the room. It felt full of buzzings, energies, vectors.

Two microphones set up in the middle of the room, at either end of the walkway, for audience participation. Those with a question or comment approached the microphone and stood in line, and then negotiated taking turns speaking, merging onto the freeway. Sometimes the merging didn't go well, and people spoke over one another or deferred to one another or didn't. One had to take up a lot of space and present one's body at the microphone to speak. It seemed humiliating, the idea of standing there waiting. The same cars kept getting on the freeway. When the car was Rachel Blau DuPlessis I never minded. One of my parts was joking around in the back with the bad kids how the line for the microphone was all guys the same guys. Then Brian Kim Stefans got up and said something like "I defer to the senator from the bay area" (that's me) but I didn't actually have a question or a way to intervene. I felt embarrassed. Later in the day BKS called me a shyster. It's true, I'm shy in this room. "But not deceptively so." I perspire.

It seemed like, maybe, once someone had stood up at the microphone and spoken, it was easier to move forward in the room, to seat oneself towards the front. It seemed like, once someone had talked on a panel, it was easier to move forward in the room, towards the front. This was true for me. I sat in the box seats the afternoon after presenting on a panel, after mostly sitting in the back. This is probably a bad generalization extrapolating from my own subjectivity. But I am thinking of how Don Byrd started in the back of the room, and then by the last panel, was in the third row.

When Marjorie Perloff makes the comment, during a formalist reading of Vanessa Place's forthcoming *Statement of Facts*, that the rape victims in the book are "at least as bad as or worse than the rapists" there's this wave of faces in reaction throughout the room. The faces are audible, there are gasps. There are chins dropping. There are eyes meeting in disbelief. I'm sitting across the room, sort of in between the stage left jury box box seats and one of the microphone stands, actually right in between two covered pianos, why are there pianos in the dissertation boot camp?

Across the way is Shelagh Patterson, sitting in the front row of the stage right jury box box seats, I'm watching her face as I'm feeling my own, I sort of expect someone to stand up and shout but nobody does, not even during the Q & A, *it doesn't come up at all*. Nobody brings it up. The Q & A is entirely about genre, and form. Everybody's talking about Perloff's remark at the break, but until facebook a few days after the conference, the only public presence of this remark is Aaron Vidaver, in the #rethinkingpoetics twitter feed. When Juliana puts her hand on the Perloff comment the next morning, framing it inside a question about what seems like a shared inability or difficulty of reading content in conceptual writing (which seems distinctly related to Mónica de la Torre's talk on concrete poetry, more in a second on that) nobody takes up the opportunity to further discuss the Perloff comment. Also she, Perloff, is no longer in the room.

I'm also trying to think through the Perloff comment through the question posed by de la Torre: is the ghost of concrete poetry haunting conceptual poetry? Her talk takes up concrete poetry as a moment of, as John Keene writes "image prevailing over the text," of the medium becoming the message, and how this series of moves facilitates global export and distribution. And how in the case of concrete poetry this ease of global export, of the image, is such precisely because there is no—fuzz? glitch? disruption?—in its transmission, such that the receiver can go ahead and fill it up with what is already known, what the receiver already thinks.

The Perloff comment on Place's work seemed clearly an example of just such a haunting.

Eleni Stecopoulos (in Mark Wallace's comment box)
"More subtle but just as painful was her dismissal of the "poetics and ecology" panel, and implicitly everything the poet Sherwin Bitsui, who is Dine (Navajo), had just said about "enter[ing] poetic space" through ceremonial song, language's power, hozho. I didn't hear anyone take her on publicly about this."
Yesterday at 2:08pm

Late Saturday afternoon, Bob Perelman announces that instead of the two standing microphones, several wireless mics will instead circulate through the room, that this has been suggested as a model that might make it easier for more people to speak. This of course immediately changes who is talking. Suddenly, the graduate students. I feel so glad, more speakers, and then my heart sinks a little. The form of most questions spends 50% of their time establishing the speaker's discourse proficiency, and the remaining 50% framing a question mostly having to do with the speaker's project, related back in some baroque way (to use Brian's descriptive word for discourse at the conference) to something that had been spoken on the panel.

Brian Kim Stefans (in Mark Wallace's comment box)
But in the end everyone was very nice and it was great to catch up with

old friends. I feel a bit revitalized in a way since I'm pretty happy with my research and managed not to tell anyone about it.

Yesterday at 2:40pm

I'm grateful for moments such as when Bridget Madden asks Lisa Robertson why "we" (a "we" I took to be English-speaking students/readers/teachers of literature) aren't familiar with the French writer Henri Meschonnic, a translation of whose writing Lisa discussed and read from. Lisa says she asked Norma Cole the same thing and Norma's answer is that he didn't travel like others to the U.S. (Foucault, Derrida), didn't spend a lot of time promoting himself, "here." (Obviously an academic "here.") He stayed home and worked. Thus this "we" is unfamiliar with him.

Then I think how this "we" unfamiliar with Meschonnic probably includes many people in the room at this conference, and then also people outside of it, people in other non-academic poetic scenes. There is a "we" who is largely unfamiliar with Meschonnic. The "we" is constructed here, momentarily, around a shared gap, lack, area of not-seeing. This area probably includes more than just Meschonnic. This is probably some error in logic on my part but I am trying hard to think of alternate ways we might construct a "we" which are not necessarily built around a neutralization (or nuancing to death) of difference, but also not necessarily antagonism as the central or best generator of knowledge, identity, positionality.

I am glad Nada Gordon is in the room. How she said, on facebook, that she felt alienated in advance, and yet there she was, present and talking and questioning and being in the room. How great that is.

I'm grateful for Rodrigo's talk which begins with Guillermo Gomez-Peña, begins with re-situating the dominant framework of the room, and goes on to discuss the work of Carla Harryman, William Howe and

Suzanne Stein, a grouping of writers and thinkers who, so far as I can remember, don't show up anywhere else in the conference.

I am grateful every time someone mentions a thinker or writer who hasn't already been named into the room once or several times previously.

It's interesting when Susan Howe discusses Graham Foust. Lyric work doesn't show up very much at this academic poetics conference.

I'm grateful to Tonya Foster for her "Talking Shit" and how the form of the forgotten, the gap in the memory, is so often flushed away (after being observed, poked at, as it rests in the porcelain bowl) and how she ends instead with a model that might be "many forms floating in proximity."

I am grateful to Tonya Foster for talking about *Zong*.

Nada Gordon The whole first day of the conference I'm afraid I had a wedgie, and that had a great impact on how I perceived the proceedings.
Yesterday at 1:58pm · Comment · Like

I guess I had a wedgie the whole time.

I get home and I'm so tired, I have plans to see David Brazil & Sara Larsen on Monday night and think I'll be too exhausted but then realize I'm the kind of spiritually exhausted girl who needs to see David & Sara, like how I was always dehydrated at the academic poetics conference and each night felt like a leaf coming back to life as I drank 7 glasses of water at the restaurant. It is reminding me of another road trip Juliana and I went on together, the poetry bus fiasco, and how, like this time, Joshua was there. Jen Hofer was also on the poetry bus (but not the conference) and Jen Bervin (was in the conference room for a second and I was so happy to see her, she told me about her new puppy) and Anna (also in the conference room) and others. At the end of the poetry bus road trip we landed in Los Angeles and it just happened to be the weekend of the CalArts conference, speculations on the expanded field of writing, where I missed seeing Young-Hae Chang Heavy Industries but we rolled ourselves into a panel for maybe thirty minutes and the air conditioning was great, the ac on the bus was broken at that point, and we sat in the back row and I think we saw and heard Kasey talk there? In general it felt like such a relief, here were our people, and although of course there are similar arguments to be made about the CalArts slice, the CalArts construction of an academic poetic scene, in that moment I was grateful because it so so wasn't the poetry bus.

At David & Sara's house we talk of many things.

At the academic poetics conference, discussion of phatic language showed up a lot at after Kasey brought it up, in his fantastic egghead mini-lecture on critical traditions and semiotics. He finished with discussion of how a phatic aesthetic shows up in say, flarf, conceptual writing, noise—music?—or the work of someone like Nathaniel Mackey, but that there's no phatic critical practice showing up as yet, and what would that look like, and is it necessarily, would it necessarily be, the hiccup, the stutter?

At David & Sara's house, we talk about vatic language, and how religious grammars have in the past and in some places and some times been the grammar of social movements and revolutions.

Which is definitely not something that showed up as such at the conference, although Nada said in her comment in the Q&A after Lisa Robertson's talk on Meschonnic that she'd been wanting and waiting for the tent revival feeling, and although I think it's there, in places such as Joan Retallack's talk on poetics as "a form of courage", and ideas around reciprocal alterity, in Rachel Zolf's insistence on a poetics of witness that goes beyond a one, a witness of addition, of difference, of intersubjective contact. Or in dinner conversations where Mark Nowak talks about the Split this Rock conference and how different it was in relation to a community, or Kaplan Harris' question about activist poetries in the bay area, this kind of astonishing list of benefit readings in the 70s and early 80s, at places like Glide Memorial, or the Unitarian/Universalist Church in Berkeley, or the Burlingame Public Library, benefits for the Greek Resistance, or Chilean refugees, or the Bilateral Nuclear Weapons Freeze, and how these enormous benefit readings, in solidarity with, stopped happening in the bay area, and why?

The other thing Sara says as we are talking of many things including facebook, is how it isn't really known yet, the ways in which these corporate forms of spectacular sociability are changing the shape of consciousness, and that it is kind of the poet's job to be thinking about this, and that perhaps just signing up to swim around in these consciousness changing forms, might not be the best idea ever. And what might the shape of our criticality take. I want to kill my facebook so so badly. It makes me feel so so bad. Yet I'm addicted to its information. I locate my addiction only by way of the bad feelings. I know it makes me feel bad, and I can't as of yet stop.

Can't stop thinking how blogger, which I haven't used in a "long" time, now has a MONETIZE tab. Monetize this blog. Ariana Reines doing (among many other things) such great parodic work on this at her new blog.

The question of a reshaping of consciousness via new forms of mediation does of course show up at the conference. I'm grateful when

Charles Bernstein asks about forms of reading, such as the three-day form of listening-as-reading, which this conference has been.

I'd be curious what Sara might have had to say about this, had she been at the academic poetics conference.

The other thing David reminds me is that you have to write things down right away or you will lose them. So I start writing this thing, which is now 11 pages long, half-baked, punched through with errors.

Also, facebook is changing what I remember of the academic poetics conference, changing the way I want to talk about it, what I want to say or respond to as I'm trying to respond, I veer again and again into what's being said there, right now, for instance Jonathan Skinner is saying some smart things in the comment stream on Barrett's page.

Hi!

Some dangling pieces from my notes which I want to bring back here into a kind of visible invisibility, or sets of questions:

Elizabeth Willis invoked the figure of the preacher but I don't remember the context. ? Also from her talk, that the idea of surrender shows up in the OED definition of "tradition." Also the importance of counter-traditions.

Who talked about the "enlarged intimate addition to his memory" (the memex) Was it Kasey?

An exchange between Tonya and Ben on the traditions panel, this question of what is, who is, "we"? "Whatever is not considered we is excrement-alized."

Tonya again (and this seems to radically condense and critique the entire self-involved beginning of this 12 page deal I seem to be writing) "we can't know our obligations to one another... but partly it involves being in discomfort"

I think it is also Tonya, or maybe Elizabeth, who brings up the library, and public institutions in general, as holders of cultural authority, how we are losing these public institutions in some way, or maybe it is that the library becomes social services, and the cultural archive moves somewhere else, private or privatized.

Barrett quoting Zizek, something like "I cannot maintain my self (whole) in moments of antagonism." Antagonism as something that undoes the whole.

Monica: the hybrid is our inability to relate to complete total difference.

I write a question somewhere in my notes, maybe it is me thinking this question? How might we better understand the nature of our antagonisms. I say back to myself, the bruise, bruising channels of invisibility. I say back to myself, echolocation.

Steve and "provisionally complicit resistance"

Is it Cecil, or Mark, who says "stuff done for free in public"

Charles: "even the most isolated work is collective"

Mark, how taking a position does not equal taking an action.

(Correlative: making a shocked face does not equal taking a position.)

Rachel Blau DuPlessis makes a really helpful and concrete suggestion, about resource-sharing between UPenn and Temple University in Philadelphia, where the resource distribution is uneven.

I am realizing I have a poetics crush on Rachel BDP.

Don Byrd's many useful questions and interruptions at the microphone. Douglas also. For being sand in the vaseline of a smooth proceeding.

"the thing formerly known as the public sphere" I think that is Jeff Derksen? As he is making that super helpful list of various free schools, during his comment after the poetics & the academy panel: Copenhagen free university, Manoa free university. Kootenay.

Steve on not discounting the pleasures of thinking together, in this way. I think he means this room of the conference. Don't discount its pleasures. Steve also, that any exclusion must be able to give an accounting for itself. Or it has fallen down on the job.

Eco-poetics as a site, not a genre.

What we need is a return to amateurism!! Exclamation points mine. Quote Jonathan Skinner's.

Susan Howe, who or what was she talking about? "it seemed reckless and austere at once"

Jeff Derksen called scare quotes "scratchies." Realizing I have a poetics crush on Jeff. Along with risking a discussion of the "sincere" as a "relationship to one's own affect under conditions of neoliberalism." And sincerity as an affective "something that intervenes between the body and neoliberalism." And "the intensification of the problem of body under capitalism." And "sincerity as software that can presence the…" (my notes trail off there, after trailing ink around the page)

Need to read Aaron Vidaver's poem, "The Market Prefers"

Lisa, from the Meschonnic writing, "make a listening of us"

Also Meschonnic, from his glossary of terms:

"Historicity = the continuous addition of others to the subject" (thinking here necessarily of Rachel Zolf's talk)

Also "A poem = a continuity, an action, not an object. A straying."

And "Subject = the mode of orality."

Poetics crush on Meschonnic.

Chris Nealon talking about poetics as a rhetoric (versus a grammar— thinking here about discussion of the vatic with David, I wonder how this opposition might figure? Need to discuss.) And also poetics as rhetoric v. language and linguistics.

Talking to Ben on the last day between panels, took some mangled notes about his inhabitation of flarf, as taking one's own subject position as that which is mocked, or messed with, as a way to activate (locate?) one's subjectivity via negative affects and shame. (thinking here again about a disruption in the transmission, that this seems to be one form of disruption, Ben's model I mean.)

Talking with Laura about affect theory late late at the bar. The moment when Laura is the next person in line to ask a question after the affect panel and then the Q & A is over and out of time it is a bummer.

Asking her what her question would have been, asking her drunkenly at the bar hours later. Many moments like this. The urgency of her question.

This is the part where I am going to post my talk for the poetics & the academy panel, I am not sure what it means that I have forced/led you through these 13 pages to locate it. I am immediately full of disagreement with myself about this talk, also I think some of my critiques of Rubin are maybe too easy, and that after all there might be something very useful about rendering visible or material some of these new forms of spectacular sociability, which I think the waffle shop might be trying to do.

I think the waffle shop might be trying to be about "provisionally complicit resistance."

Also I have seriously failed if this talk transmits an insistence "on the primacy and importance of academic institutions."

I'm curious about the relations between the academic poetic scene and the non-academic poetic scene, how each scene constructs itself oppositionally, but what might its other relations be? Or what are the nature of the antagonisms between these two locations? Maybe I am more interested in this set of antagonisms than the antagonisms between a mainstream and whatever gets named experimental, probably because I so unaware of, and uninterested in, the former.

Another question I have and is how might the academic institution put itself in service to locations that are not itself, but without the often bad politics of "service learning" which is too often finally about institutional outcomes.

There are other things I've gotten wrong. Here is the talk.

Panel Description:

Given that higher education in the US is more or less a pay to play system (whether one pays with cash or with labor), one extensively supported by a governmental credit baiting student loan system; given its somewhat feudal hiring and retention practices and the difficulties of getting more than two aligned colleagues in one location; given that the possibility of teaching creative writing is frequently denied or belittled by the very people who are hired to teach it; and yet despite all this, given that the higher education system unfortunately and ironically remains both one of the more progressive and richest institutions in the US, is there anything that we, whatever "we" are, can do with or within this higher education system all together? The larger question might be: should there, could there, be an inter/national Poetics Program? If there were, what would it do? How would it do it? But perhaps the easier way to get at these questions is to rethink the conventions around those ways that poetry and poetics enters the academy: the reading series, the talk series, the conference, the seminar restricted to those who are paying to attend the university, the writers center/house, the summer program, the workshop, etc.

I want to start with the confession that, big surprise, my thinking here is inflected by the bay area, with its many graduate programs in creative writing and its deeply engaged non-institutionally affiliated poetry communities, and then the variously overlapping, murky, unpredictable, parasitic, and sometimes antagonistic relations between these locations, between these many academic creative writing programs and local poetry communities. These locations and relationships are where I work, at a small, gated private college situated between some poor neighborhoods and some middle-class neighborhoods in Oakland, with very rich neighborhoods just up the hill. I have one of these odd hybrid non-contractual but impossible to lose jobs, as the full-time coordinator/admin in the graduate creative writing program, and seemingly permanent part-time adjunct faculty in the undergraduate creative writing program. And one part of this job is curating, somewhat by committee, the reading series at the college, where I work with Juliana, and whenever she and I are sitting and eating lunch in one of our offices, or walking around the fenced perimeter of the college, hatching plots designed to push the workshops, curriculum or reading series at this gated private college to operate in intellectually meaningful or provocative ways that might go beyond the generally low requirements and expectations of the creative writing program, and which might also be intellectually meaningful or provocative to a community larger than the one composed of those whose money and thus selves circulate through the fenced campus, in these conversations, I often want to bring up Jon Rubin as a useful figure to think through or around.

Rubin ran the ISA, independent school of art, in San Francisco several years ago during, as a writer at a local group blog describes it, an "ambivalent stint as a teacher at the San Francisco Art Institute." The school operated autonomously without external resources, accreditation, or a physical site. Tuition was by barter; every admitted student was given the same first assignment of making $100 in a week without getting a job. There were plans for a department of continuing education after Rubin left for his current tenure track assistant professor position at Carnegie Mellon, but so far as I can tell the ISA no longer exists, except as a project on Rubin's CV. In an interview with him in 2006 before he left the bay area, we talked about the importance of the ISA's nomadic qualities, "a pedagogical situation that I felt was healthy for an art school and its students to negotiate. There are plenty of resources out there already that we just co-op for our use, from living rooms and restaurants to empty school classrooms and under-attended art galleries." I'm guessing some of those re-directed resources for the independent school of art arose from Rubin's association with the art institute; and imagine it might be easier to redirect the resources of an institution one has an ambivalent and casual / non-contractual relationship to. Many of Rubin's projects have utilized state/institutional funds to build structures that facilitate temporary barter systems intended to make obscured resources and connections available to members of a given community: the Seattle Arts Commission-funded FREEMOBILE in 2003 is a good example; he modified a 1968 Chevy step-van which then toured through one south Seattle neighborhood each weekend, driven by a different neighborhood resident each time, who distributed something free to their neighbors, from hand-printed t-shirts to bike repair, dance lessons, bird calls and personalized poetry.

So I've been intensely curious what's happened since Rubin and his projects have been tethered, via tenure, to Carnegie Mellon. The most visible project (on the internet) is the waffle shop, located off university property in a formerly vacant storefront, now a restaurant serving 4$ waffles and producing and broadcasting a live-streaming talk show with its customers. The waffle shop runs a take-out window called the Conflict Kitchen (which sometimes goes out into greater Pittsburgh as a takeout cart) that sells food from countries "engaged in conflict with the U.S." Unlike the independent school of art, the waffle shop is a permanent location, and while its goal is co-production of culture within the larger Pittsburgh community, it seems symptomatic of what happens when collectively-organized and relationally-driven projects move into the university and become somewhat stuck. Where the Independent School of Art talked of resource redirection in a vague way without naming the location or owners of those resources, the waffle shop has a long list of funders and sponsors, both non- and for profit, including Whole Foods and several urban redevelopment companies in Pittsburgh. Where Rubin's pre-Carnegie Mellon projects could best be described as nomadic, collective, temporary models of the possible, the tenured professor at Carnegie Mellon model is one of cottage industry and small business; Rubin describes it thusly on the

Carnegie Mellon website: "Building an interior deals with sculpture and commerce. We're designing promotional materials, painting signs, editing video, as well as running a small business—we deal with a lot of skill sets. Just in making the talk show, you're pulling upon performance, writing, acting, and constructing social situations, which is an art process in itself."

I recognize here the sorts of language necessary to represent and sell a project back to its sponsoring institution and so I also recognize the ways in which something that has certain stakes when operating outside of an institution is so often reduced in the university to a set of marketable, professional skills and pre-digested knowledge. As a university-funded location, the project's central goals are necessarily student-oriented; in my internet tour of the waffle shop it wasn't clear how the project might be useful to the community it's situated in, beyond presenting a set of perhaps unrealized potentials. The talk show routinely asks skyped in visitors the most banal questions—which three people from history would you most want to hang out with, etc. The conflict kitchen seems arbitrary at worst and cavalier at best, especially when considered in contrast to 2003's freemobile which was literally driven by neighborhood residents. Yet it's no small thing, convincing a university to support and develop offsite pedagogical and programming space which moves students off campus, and into relationship with the neighborhoods and people the university is part of. I ran across a great quote from a recent talk by Rubin, where he proposed three big ideas for Pittsburgh: the installation of giant fans around the perimeter of Pittsburgh, to drive clouds away and create permanently sunny weather conducive to business and tourism, exporting the Steelers as an off-season touring soccer team, and kicking all of Pittsburgh's universities out of their buildings and relocating them into "apartments, storefronts, boats and tree houses."

And so, some questions:

I wonder what would happen if every college and university reading series kicked itself out of the lecture hall or student union or lobby come living room where it usually takes place?

Is it even possible to move the university reading series off campus? What does it say that it might not even be?

This question of course means differently across locations, and depends a lot on the relationship of individual institutions to local communities, geography, etc.

In the Bay Area it is often the case that a poet comes from New York and reads at 5:30 on a Tuesday at Mills, 6:30 on a Wednesday at UC Berkeley, 4:30 on a Thursday at the Poetry Center, and then at 7:30 on Friday night at SPT and/or 7:00 on Sunday Night at 21 Grand. The university series will all be attended almost entirely by students at each individual institution, and the local poetry community will come out on a Friday or Sunday to SPT or 21Grand. In this case the reader benefits from the combined honoraria and travel fees cobbled together from each location, the students and faculty at each individual institution ostensibly benefit from this interaction with the contemporary, and the poetry community benefits by a reading from someone who might not have had the financial resources to come out otherwise. At no point, however, will these separate audiences encounter one other. In this and other ways they come to believe they are not necessarily in relationship.

I keep wondering what might happen, how might it happen, that the institutional reading series might imagine its commitments as larger than the benefit of students, faculty, and individual institutional brands.

What would happen if all the institutional locations got together and, say, pooled their money.

What would happen if, for one year, there was a single university reading series in the Bay Area, which every institution contributed budget $$ to, and MFA students in every program were required to attend at a location off campus? My guess is that there are at least 250 MFA students in the bay area at any given moment, maybe up to 350. What would happen if that group of students encountered itself as a larger group, and came into continued forms of contact and relation?

What would happen if that university reading series, with its pooled funds and single series on campus, was scheduled at a time and location highly congenial to those who aren't students, say at 8:00?

What would happen if each visiting writer was charged with the task of imagining and experimenting with a possible or potential relationship the institution might have with a local community beyond students and faculty or even poets?

What would happen if each visiting writer was charged with the task of reimagining the role of programs such as poets in the schools?

What would happen if the reading series became a seminar open both to students and larger community, for whom it would be free, and the seminar met before each reading? What if part of reading series budget was committed to build and publicize this free seminar program?

What would happen if, instead of reader suggestions coming from faculty at each institution, all suggestions for readers were solicited by members of the writing community outside of the institution?

What would happen if the university reading series partnered w. non-institutional reading series each year and is in this way was covertly curated by, or in collaboration with, those non-institutional partners?

In short, how might we redirect the resources of host institutions? Probably I am also trying to say something quickly here about individual identifications with power, particularly in a moment of profound transition from a largely tenured workforce to departments running on 50% + adjunct labor. The struggle to get inside an institution can make it profoundly difficult to untangle one's attachments once one is inside, to do more than discharge institutional requirements. And yet those who are only provisionally inside these institutions have far less power to push something like the reading series beyond its given, AWP-required formal minimums.

If these questions seem perhaps impoverished, not as expansive as they might be, allow me to relate a recent scheduling moment for the Mills reading series, wherein I was working with Samantha Giles at Small Press Traffic to schedule a reading with Hiromi Ito, who couldn't be in town long enough to read at Mills on a Tuesday and SPT on a Friday. Samantha suggested a co-sponsored reading at a location off the Mills and CCA campuses (SPT is housed at CCA, a good example of academic and non-academic entanglement) and when Samantha suggested this, my first thought was: that's impossible.

MUTUAL AID

When you're writing in real time, you have to revise a lot. In the summer of 2010, in anticipation of the Mehserle verdict, Oakland police participated in riot training. They called it crowd control, they called it a massive exercise. You can watch on the local news, archived on YouTube. ABC Channel 7. Otherwise it's difficult to find a trace, that ramp-up to the verdict, in shot after shot a shop owner boards up the windows. In training, police circle a small group of people sitting on the ground, arms linked, backs touching. The simulated riot. Police circle, raise and smash batons through air, it's like watching *Stomp!* Batons pause, hover over the small group sitting on the ground. The simulated riot. *That's right…today's massive exercise was designed to make sure that Oakland is ready if and when there is more rioting.* Arms linked, batons smashing. 150 Oakland police participated in the exercise, plus 200 officers from "other agencies," the Highway Patrol, Fire Department. *This is a refresher course we'll call it, and make sure everybody has their equipment, make sure it all works, and make sure that everybody remembers exactly how crowd, uh, control techniques work.*

Every time you try and write the truth it changes. More happens. Information constantly expands. Were 80 people arrested on or after the July 8, 2010 demonstration following the Mehserle verdict? Or was it 90? 78? It's later now; I can't figure it out. It is difficult to get the news, period. People die miserably every day. Some die more than others, some die more miserably. Somewhere in my earlier notes I indicate that 19 of those arrested on July 8 were from California, but outside the Bay Area, 12 were from out of state, and "the rest were from local cities." Where did I get this information? That would mean 49, or 59, or 47 of those arrested were from the Bay Area, depending on the total number of arrests. Would mean 60% were from the Bay Area, that more of those arrested on July 8 were from the Bay Area than not. And yet, at a press conference following the protest, the Oakland chief of police said that nearly 3 out of 4 of those arrested "did not live in Oakland."

As if BART trains only ran through Oakland and no further.

As if the borders between cities were real.

Under the borders, the fault. The Hayward about 74 miles long, running through Richmond and El Cerrito, Berkeley and Oakland, San Leandro and Hayward. Merging east of San Jose with the Calaveras, a major branch of the San Andreas, principal transform boundary between the Pacific and North American Plates. The divergent, convergent, and transform boundaries. Where plates pull away from or dive under each other as crust is destroyed and recycled back into the earth. Where plates slide horizontally past one another.

What was I doing in the summer of 2010 while the OPD trained to riot, while a jury found Johannes Mehserle guilty of involuntary manslaughter and not guilty of both the second-degree murder and voluntary manslaughter charges? Mostly I was planning a party. A wedding. My own. Mostly I felt excited and tender and anxious. Ambivalent about the institution. I purchased a lot of shoes online while I tried to write about the problems of gender and the law in a letter to Clive I guess I called marriage a technology? I guess I was using that word a lot. The shoes were ugly and overpriced. I returned them. Meanwhile we felt excited and tender and anxious and stockpiled wine. After going back and forth we reserved Sequoia Lodge, where years earlier the wake for Clive's father was held. It felt right. Our dead fathers in the room. During the week, Sequoia Lodge is a pre-school. On weekends the city rents it out for parties. Families fall apart and still keep going.

Our mostly middle class friends the poets and actors and teachers and theater board members volunteered everything, picked up ice and buckets, cut and arranged flowers from the wholesale mart in donated vases, served champagne on trays, brought duraflame logs for a fireplace in the conversation pit. In the summer of 2010 I signed every email THANK YOU, or THANK YOU SO MUCH. I happily volunteered the party's final price tag to anyone who seemed interested. After all, our guests were the ones who made it possible to spend what seemed so little. I volunteered this information the same way I can never stop myself from asking how much money my friends earn at their jobs, or how much the unemployment check is for. The mortgage payment. The wedding cost $7,000 in the end, $5,000 of it from my mother. $7,000 is simultaneously a very small and very large amount of money to spend on a wedding. It depends on how you look at it. From what vantage point.

In a photo from the party my friends the mostly middle class poets are dressed in shades of mauve and tan and gold. They are dapper in fedoras, in white and brown and black suit coats, in pink and blue shirts, in yellow shoes and green and white and black and white dresses. They are beautiful in floppy-brimmed farmer hats. In shirt-sleeves and jewelry. Patterned tights.

After the first conference and before the second, the community poetics and labor conference, I was mostly preoccupied with this party. Excited and tender and anxious. I signed all my emails THANK YOU. Or THANK YOU SO MUCH. I thought about the problems of the first conference a little less. Still, when I read the announcement for the second conference on the internet and learned of the decision made by my friends, the organizers, to invite as presenters only poets who did not work inside the academy, I got hot all over. Biopsychosocial distress. On facebook. In the comment stream. Tonya Foster says "Whatever is not considered we is excrement-alized." That sounds melodramatic or at least incommensurate with the situation. But it's true, I felt like shit. I is the conditions of my labor didn't belong anywhere. Not in New York, and not in Oakland.

I kept getting tangled in these local arguments about the academy that showed up around both conferences, kept shouting stuff about spreadsheets, or muttering to myself, BUT I'M LIKE YOU, in the office 9-5, two things in my job, administrator and adjunct, feet snagged in these arguments, who were they even for? Arguments about power and visibility, for example inequities between Jackie and Gilles, the latter who often travelled to give readings and talks at other universities, professional commitments expected of him as a full professor, while Jackie, a poet who worked at the library, did not. The academic institutions where Gilles spoke generally paid significant honoraria along with covering full travel costs. While both Jackie and Gilles were often invited to read at community institutions in other cities which paid little or no honoraria, Gilles was able to afford the travel costs of these unpaid readings because of other honoraria he received throughout the year, along with limited travel funds available to tenured faculty at the university where he worked, whereas Jackie had for many years charged her poetry-related travel costs, eventually maxing out her credit cards, and now more often than not declined invitations to speak or read in other cities because she could not afford to do so.

In his talk at the second conference, Steve characterized the labor conditions of those who work in the academy: *all that time to write*. I stared ahead red-faced through this idea as it firmed up in the room as given. That this idea seemed more true of academic labor 30 years ago, and applied now to such a small percentage of academic jobs as to be anecdotal, mythic, individual, didn't enter the conversation. The local arguments valorized the outside of the poetry community, the freedom of that. You can write what you want on the outside, in the community, but not if you work in the academy. You may have more time in the academy, but you're trapped. All of this seemed both true and not true, and anyways the academy changing so much, so fucked up, so many different things and workers, it's difficult to say "academy" without description or qualification, it's like saying "community," you can't assume anyone else's understanding of the word corresponds with your own. Anyways, I was more concerned with, I am trying to test, what I can and can't write in the community, the scene, the mostly middle class poets I am and hang out with.

I was both sides of something. As were so many others. I kept explaining. It made for a lot of prepositions, a lot of p sounds. Provisional labor. People slipped through the borders of the second conference anyways. Many presenters were or had been adjunct faculty at local community colleges and private colleges and public universities, sometimes in addition to or alongside other work they did for wages. So often the boundary wasn't visible until it slipped. So often the boundary wasn't visible because adjunct faculty labor conditions were so bad. The privileges associated with tenure applied to so few of the mostly middle class poets I am and hang out with. You could count them on one hand. Which is part of what made something about the second conference feel so personal. And yet the overall privilege of everyone in this paragraph, of those who work inside and those who work outside the academy, the overall privilege of the mostly middle class poets I am and hang out with is staggering if you begin to look past the borders of the group that convened in Oakland at a community arts center to hear some of us, invited by others of us, speak mostly about our individual work lives, working for wages outside the academy.

It was not as if the antagonism were not real, if also somewhat murky. Not as if MFA programs in creative writing had not grown from 15 in 1975 to 184 in 2010. The mostly middle class poets I am and hang out with found one another in a moment where it felt important to insist again and again that nobody needs a degree to be a poet, most poets do not hold tenured teaching jobs, that the pipeline from degree to degree to publication to job was in fact broken, the boom only a blip in the long history of poets and poetry. Or it felt important to me, in my job in the bubble, which involved meeting with prospective MFA students to answer their questions about the creative writing program.

On the phone, in my office, I felt bound to say aloud what more and more prospective MFA students understood already: that the terminal degree in creative writing offers no guaranteed employment outcome other than teaching, and every year the 184 programs produce far more graduates than tenure track teaching jobs. As MFA graduates increase and tenure disappears, the handful of positions available each year increasingly require both the MFA and PhD. That one should think carefully before accruing so much debt. Which is not to say one could not learn a great deal in an MFA program in creative writing, could not grow as a writer; make new friends. One might even, if the stars of tuition and annual loan caps aligned, and perhaps with the help of a spouse's salary or small amount left by a great-aunt, get two years off the job market altogether, two years to write, to grow as a writer; make new friends. At this point in the conversation the other part of me would go on to discuss amenities students could expect for such a price. I was mostly unable to get into the more complicated part, how creative writing programs professionalized and replicated work done by communities so often for so long for nothing, or love, or small amounts of government funding. How the programs tended to monetize complicated friendship as networking. Privatize a community art form.

It was impossible to say and harder to see how all this might have a particular impact on the mostly middle class poets I am and hang out with, what impact on our friendships and reading groups, kissing and petting, free chapbooks and house readings. Everything that kept going, everything we did for love, for nothing, the little magazines, the reading series in someone's living room, ourselves, even—after the second conference I felt it all shot through with shards of competition. Something felt ruined.

Does that sound naïve? Let's say I knew it intellectually before the second conference. Afterwards I felt it in my ribs, and all along my face. I remember Taylor saying something during the discussion period, like it might be useful to be interpellated in such a way. I'm not sure which way he meant. For sure I felt interpellated.

Still I kept wondering why my friends the organizers found it necessary to foreground the exclusion of some members of a community on the basis of their individual jobs. Couldn't my friends the organizers have invited the same group of poets to discuss the relation of their labor and writing without naming the criteria of exclusion? Maybe naming this criteria was a response to the academy's unarticulated but given exclusion of those not running its game. But couldn't the community do more than the academy? Wasn't it wider? Wasn't that sort of the point? I wasn't sure anymore: the exclusion blotted my view, what I could and couldn't see, the antagonism between individuals who work inside and outside the academy, tech writers and adjunct comp instructors, bartenders and creative writing faculty. It felt counter-productive. I mean to me. Inside my body. Inside a small community which at the same time seemed to be thinking together in pairs and groups more and more, and more and more about radical history and social movements. Labor. Resistance. Solidarity. While at the same time some of its members, students and faculty at the University of California at Davis, at Berkeley, at Santa Cruz, were striking and occupying buildings in protest of the intense fee hikes that would effectively privatize what remained of California's public university system.

That many of the middle class poets I am and hang out with might have enjoyed a robust fantasy life in relation to the pipeline only a few years earlier, when the fantasy around the pipeline was still intact, that some of us might have imagined particular returns on our educational investment and debt, we didn't speak of. We didn't speak of pipelines or booms or blips or bubbles at all. And neither did we speak of NAFTA, or the real estate market, or cuts to public education, or plus loans, everything that made earlier fantasy lives impossible, perhaps the lives we mourned most of all, the lost bohemia Michael Gottlieb describes in *Lives of the Poets*, living like "a slightly well-off undergraduate—one step up from that especially luxurious poverty—for twenty years or more." At the second conference, convened in a small room at a community arts center, the mostly middle class poets I am and hang out with came together to hear some of us, invited by others of us, speak mostly about our individual work lives, of being individual poets who worked for wages outside the academy. We didn't speak of these wages in particular, didn't name salaries or benefit packages, how weird it was that some of us who spoke or were invited to speak might make $35,000 annually as administrative assistants, while others might take home $70,000 or more in the tech industry, while still others relied on tips, or what about the ones who slipped through, did they earn $3,500 for each section of composition, or $5,000 for beginning fiction, or $70,000 annually as tenured faculty? Who had health insurance with a PPO and who was on the high deductible plan with Kaiser and who had no insurance and why?

At the second conference I sat in the small room at the community arts center with my body held very still, looking straight ahead. I felt as if I had to sit there and *take it*. I is the conditions of my labor didn't belong anywhere. Waves of sweat ripping up my ribcage. My face very hot. I ate handfuls of snacks at the break, pretzels and chocolate, shoveled it in and didn't talk about whatever it was that felt so personal, I took something personally, something ripping or tearing in the body, in the family, in the home sort of, in the guts. In the guts of the room, of the organs that matter—to our bodies, the organs our bodies are made of. I went back and forth on this. Whose body was whose. Was it one big body like a church. I didn't mean to presume you are part of me. I didn't mean to presume I am part of you. But secretly, I felt this was true.

That the central forms of my childhood should provide the vocabulary through which to describe this profound discomfort at the conference came as no surprise. The church, the family embedded in the church, the stories told there about women and what they can do—such was the shape of feeling as if I had to sit there and *take it*, the shape of shoveling it in, of obscured ambivalence in the thing I made that failed, what I couldn't write, didn't know how, the shape of feelings that are the opposite of love but also love.

Dana Ward says "I wish poets were as good / at poetry as they are at resentment." Maybe one problem of the poetry scenes I'm part of is how easy they are to make all about oneself. And then you think it's not about me, and push yourself out of yourself because who wants to be stuck there, and so you look outward and it's easy then to see the group, maybe too easy to see the politics of its being together, who and what is visible there, who and what isn't, and why, which is not an unimportant thing to look at, but it's easy to get stuck there, to make it all about the group, the politics of cultural production inside a small community of the mostly middle class poets I am and hang out with.

You're not a poet till you blab about it. I'm so often pushed out of shape, jealous, shattered, hurt, I'm so *involved*, it takes up so much space. Like Dick, the community never asked me to throw myself at it. I made a scene. I lost it. I was a little lapdog. Like Dodie says "there it is, my knee-jerk eagerness to make it all about me, to activate my inner sonar that's always scanning for rejection and marginalization. Beep beep NOT ABOUT ME beep beep."

Jennifer Moxley says "the local wants to distract you into forgetting there is a world."

On November 5, 2010, Johannes Mehserle was sentenced to two years with double credit for time already served.

After the verdict was announced, people gathered at Frank Ogawa Plaza in Oakland. An altar was built. People made art, and speeches. Sang songs, read poetry, held signs. I know at least two of my friends some poets were there. Maybe more, probably more.

Where was I? Was I at work? Was I reloading the page, clicking for mobile uploads on facebook, looking for images from the rally? Was I too tired? Was my heart heavy? Was I watching the news? Was I railing at the screens, the local affiliates, diagrams representing police on the move with white x's, protesters with yellow o's, circled, surrounded, so like the play by play illustrations of football? What did I do in the fall of 2010 anyways?

Mostly, I made a patio with Clive, in the dirt and trash behind our house. The thing we made together after the party, after we got married. Made it with bricks that used to be a chimney at my friend's house. Such tenderness I felt towards these bricks, burned on one side, mortared on the other. We trundled loads from the backyard on Blake Street in two blue wheelbarrows, down the narrow walkway to the street, then stacked them in the back of a truck owned by one of the day laborers we paid to help. $200. Three truckloads back and forth between houses, and by afternoon the whole lot swayed unevenly in a pile at the end of our driveway. At the end of each workday that August, Clive and I put on our gloves and dust masks and chipped mortar from the side of each brick, one by one with special mortar-chipping tools. Placed them back in a stack with the rest. We watered the dirt, and dug into it with our shovels. Excavated plastic toys, broken pipes, knobs, wheels. We bought sand. I missed the second day of the second conference because on Labor Day we laid the bricks in the ground by hand, and without intending it a pattern emerged where some bricks went in burnt side up. Our neighbor Rhee was so proud of us. She brought over a plate of barbecue.

The whole time, I felt hot all over. I felt like shit. As we trundled bricks and sat side by side on the bench chipping mortar, breathing through our masks, while we dug a hole in the dirt and trash and got down on our knees to lay each piece of my friend's former chimney in the ground, I talked with Clive about the conferences. Especially Labor Day. I talked about it a lot with him because I didn't know how to talk about it in semi-public. I could talk about it with one or two of my friends, but I couldn't figure out how to talk about it with one or two of my other friends, the organizers. Until I did, and made a mess.

All of this felt very different from the academic poetics conference, which, even though I had attended and presented there in June, seemed far away and *not me*. I was this weird mole. I was *outside*. A weird mole could engage and argue about the academic poetics conference in semi-public, could talk about it with her friends, could even make new friends as she kept talking.

Whereas the second conference seemed close to me, my body, my family, in the home sort of, in the guts of the room, of the organs that matter, the organs our bodies are made of. But I is the conditions of my labor felt pushed out of its circumference. Forlorn. I is the conditions of my labor inside the academy was outside. It didn't feel good. I didn't belong anywhere.

After Clive and I finished the patio, we sat on it. I talked about the conferences some more. I was so upset. I wrote a poem about the patio, which was also a poem about the conferences. Clive began to show some small signs of fatigue with this topic. He started writing a song all about talking about conferences. We sang together on the patio while he played ukulele: *first there was a conference, and then there was a conference about the conference yeah, we conferred about the conference, and the conference about the conference, we had ourselves a conference.*

This song made me laugh, sitting on the patio in the dark, but it couldn't solve any of my problems. I wished to share this song with my friends, but no.

YEAR OF CANDOR.

At the rally on November 5, 2010, after the verdict was announced, after the altar was constructed, after the speeches and singing, after the poetry, after the crowd was no longer allowed to use its sound system in public, around 6:00 on November 5 people began to march through downtown Oakland towards Fruitvale BART station. *Two years is bullshit.* Marched down 14th until they reached Laney College, *no justice, no peace,* surrounded by police, rows of them, so many police from outside Oakland, ready to go, ready to control the crowd, ready for a massive exercise, blocking them in, 150 people barricaded within 2 residential blocks. *Let us go, we're leaving, we're leaving together* but they didn't, weren't allowed to. Only the media could leave. The observer, the person with a camera who could pass. On IndyBay, Lynda Carson reported from her window on the corner of 8th Ave. and E. 19th St., "Both men and women were running by, and some were in their teens, but most of them were in their 20's and 30's, and a few were older. A mix mostly of blacks, latinos and whites. Many were on bicycles. I could see the look of sweat and fear on peoples faces as they silently ran by trying to find a safe place to hide." In the videos things start to break down when there's nowhere to go, nobody's allowed to leave, trapped in a two block radius, all you can hear for a while is *ASSHOLE* over and over again *ASSHOLE* then *WE ARE ALL OSCAR GRANT.*

In the videos—I'm writing about something I saw on the internet.

People asked for water and were refused. A policeman poured out a bottle of water on the ground in front of someone, and laughed. One arrestee urinated on herself after multiple requests for access to a toilet. Access to prescription medication was denied. A woman with cancer requested adequate space in a holding cell so that she could lie down, she was feeling sick from chemotherapy and radiation treatments, and was refused. A woman had an asthma attack. "You should have thought about that before you got arrested."

There's no reason I couldn't have been there. But I wasn't.

Is that even true? Lil Wayne says "I stink because I have a lot of shit on my mind," and mine was obviously very full of thoughts about poets. My relationship to other poets. Poets and conferences, friendship and generosity, envy and betrayal. Wages and discipline. Bohemia lost. I found it difficult to think of much else.

The weird thing is I never even performed the thing that failed in the Bay Area: that's not entirely true. I felt like shit. I couldn't *not* perform it. I got hot all over. Biopsychosocial distress. I avoided activities that might make it worse. I didn't feel like going to readings. The more I withdrew, the worse I felt. I performed the thing that failed all the time, the obscured ambivalence part, the tension, the feelings that are the opposite of love but also love. Especially after a few glasses of wine. There was something worm-like, helpless in the way I couldn't stop. I'd wake in the morning uneasily, hands to my head, what had I done? It hurt to talk, and it hurt not to talk. I couldn't un-excrement-alize myself. I didn't know how to go forward, and I couldn't go back.

BLACK SWAN

After the second conference, I would be cast in the role of a young dancer with a prestigious New York City ballet company. I would be cast in the role of the mother, a former dancer now amateur artist, whose career ended at 28 when she became pregnant. I would be cast in the role of the exotic beauty who is more in touch with her sensuality. I would be cast in the role of the director, a cruel and demanding genius who would sleep with the ingenue. I would be cast in the role of someone selected to compete for the part alongside several other dancers. I would be cast in the role of someone who bites the director, and/or doesn't get along with the other dancers. I would be cast in the role of the aging principal dancer. My rigid technique would make me the ideal choice, but I would also lack the passion required by this role.

I would practice all the time. I would become increasingly paranoid. I would get drunk and yell, with dark makeup all around my eyes. I would barricade myself in my room. I would become increasingly critical. I would tell her how pretty she is, and carefully pull mittens over her hands before bed so that she does not hurt herself. I would sing her a lullaby. I would see my own image everywhere. I would be annoyed with her. I would paint picture after picture of the person I loved and hated. I would get a rash. I would get into an accident. I would eat the cake offered to me, although I did not want it. I would injure myself. I would hallucinate that I am having sex with my friend, and during this scene there would be a ripping, chewing sound. The scene is obviously misogynist. But it felt so real. I would peel skin away from my fingernails in long strips. It would happen in the bathroom. My friend would perform my role in my absence. I would perform my friend's role in her absence. I would sleep with the director. I would wish to sleep with the director. I would be left alone in the building.

I would betray my friend. My friend would betray me. I would feel the envy and aggression of others keenly. I would feel envious and aggressive towards others. I would seem rather childish. I would be rigid and controlling. I would pass out. I would scratch my back until it bled, and wear clothing designed to cover these scratches. I would not be part of the group. I would discover her in my room, wearing my costume. I would congratulate her, kiss her, shove her into the mirror and hide her body. Only then would I notice my own wound. Crying as I watched her performance.

THE GOLDEN HANDCUFFS

The more I thought about the conferences, the more I wrote. Letters I didn't send, or thought to send but then retracted. Pages of prose. Extended and withdrawn. The writing consisted of a sturdy nylon tape that contains small teeth running down one side, and a ratchet with small teeth housed in a small open case. The ratchet is molded to allow downward pressure to be placed upon it as the tape is threaded through the open case, then springing back up to position as the valleys of the tape align with the teeth of the ratchet, locking the zip tie.

Patti Smith has a chapbook about Houdini. A long poem about Houdini. I couldn't write any poems. Not one. No music. The more I wrote about the conferences, the more I thought about the thing I made that failed and the sound nobody recognized. The thing I made that failed Oscar Grant. The whole project. Everything I wrote before. The thing. The mostly white, mostly middle class poets I am and hang out with. Clive said *write about what delights you*, but nothing delighted me. What delighted me previously only got stuck in the small teeth of my writing and thinking now. Intuitively I felt my way through this problem must be forward, and yet any forward movement further tightened the teeth of the ratchet on the tape. Backwards movement locked it. I couldn't find the key to unlock the ratchet and start over, and neither was I flexible enough to reverse the position of my hands in relation to this writing of small teeth and nylon tape threaded through an open case. I didn't have a pen knife or a lighter. I didn't know enough to keep my hands, arms and shoulders as relaxed as possible, or to use gentle shoulder rotations to keep the blood moving. I didn't know to go down on my knees and bend my head forward so that my hands rest on my back.

Increasingly I felt the way through my problem might involve something other than more writing, something more than more thinking through writing. If I were in the back of a crowded truck or on a bus with others right now, instead of at my desk, I might grow so sweaty I could slip out of the problem for a while. I might feel like singing along in that situation. But I worried that I might also be unable to breathe, might panic, like the anxiety attacks I used to have on BART. Even thinking about those, or researching this language about zip tie handcuffs on the internet right now, further tightened the teeth of the ratchet on the tape, until I could barely think or write at all.

POST CAMP MESSIANISM

On October 30, 2007, a magnitude 5.6 earthquake struck the Calaveras Fault in Alum Rock Park near San Jose, close to where the Hayward Fault diverges from it. 2007 is the year my father died, a number, a date, I can never remember. It happened so fast. Diagnosed in 2006, I can only say what sounds untrue, worn through with repetition, that time lay suspended as I stood there by my desk, feeling the two story building above me sway from side to side, the ground rolling, as I sat next to the bed holding a sponge to his mouth. This quake knocked some groceries off the shelf. The ground rolled in an almost pretty way that October, so different from a much smaller earthquake on the Hayward earlier that same year, it struck at 3 or 4 in the morning, ruptures on the Hayward always feel like a truck running into the building, running through. A train. Death when it came due to liver failure was a kind of coma, he was gone but the struggle to go remained. Ativan on drip. My sister missed it, she was on her way. The room smelled, and he whimpered with the struggle of it. Later my mother and I stroked his thick dark hair and wailed, he had the most beautiful hair, my sister got it, with a white streak through the crown. As we wailed I experienced myself the image of a female mourner in a procession but it was only the three of us. My mother couldn't stop talking about his skin as the jaundice drained away. The whites of his eyes, white again. The room smelled so bad. I called my friend on the phone immediately, did you feel that? I talked on the phone with a representative from the organ donation center. They would take his eyes. It didn't matter about the jaundice.

I spent my nights sleeping in the basement room that used to be my sister's. Spent my nights sleeping in the small ground-level studio on Lester Ave., up the street from Lake Merritt. The basement room at my parent's house with window wells full of leaves. The studio on the ground floor built into the sloping curve of Lester Ave., with two apartments above and the building's basement directly behind the wall I pushed my bed against. After he died my mother learned how to clean leaves from window wells, pay bills, turn on the computer. Mostly I slept in the studio alone. It seemed fine to push the bed against the wall.

The night before he died I woke up in the basement room that used to be my sister's drenched in post-dream sweat. The dream of being locked in a nameless room underground. A cave. After the smallish quake on the Hayward that felt like a train running through the room, I lay in my bed in the studio on Lester Ave., thinking about the basement just beyond the wall my bed was pushed against. The unsupported support walls. Drenched in post-earthquake sweat. After a while, I got up and went to the hospital. After a while, I got up and made some tea.

Which is when my research started in earnest, with soil liquefaction and seismic intensity distribution maps, simulation videos, average time between major events, soft story buildings. I'd already lived in the area for ten years when I started obsessing on probabilities and predictions for water supply and wastewater facilities, petroleum fuel and communications networks after a 7.5 scenario on the Hayward Fault. Ground failure all along the BART lines in Richmond and Berkeley, Oakland and Hayward, Union City and Fremont, the trains running through the reddest part of these maps, the most intense area of shaking intensity, the red line in Oakland dividing black flatlands from the white foothills and hills.

More and more I thought about the transbay tube, the BART tunnel running beneath the bay. So far down. Under all that water. My research and then imagination filled the space my body, increasingly, could not travel—somewhere between Oakland and San Francisco, as the train descended into the tube, as my ears popped as the pressure changed, I experienced a sense of impending doom or death, rapid heart rate, sweating, shortness of breath, hot flashes, abdominal cramping, chest pain, dizziness, faintness, tightness in my throat, and difficulty swallowing. The tunnel under the bay held a lot of material. I crammed a lot into it. I talked about my research constantly, passed it on like a virus. At parties, at readings, standing in the hall outside my office. How the tunnel was built above ground, and submerged later. How it had grown stiff with age, how its design lagged behind conditions. People reminded me of the bridge during the Loma Prieta in 1989, how sections just dropped out, cars skidding over the edge into water so far below, and this long drop sounded fantastic, exhilarating in contrast to the dream of being trapped in a nameless room underground.

And even though the earthquake had obviously come and gone in Oakland, over and over again in so many places, it was still easier for me to imagine the earthquake that is coming, a 7.5 scenario on the Hayward Fault, system that fails in a major way every 140 years and not since 1868. Even though the earthquake had already come and gone where I lived, with uneven resource distribution, development and redevelopment, come and gone with budgets and highway construction, militarized police forces and supermax prisons, come and gone with contracting and sub-contracting, and sub-sub-contracting, I couldn't always see it. I found it so much easier to imagine the earthquake that is coming. Probably because I spent so much time browsing images of other earthquakes online; the Great Hanshin Earthquake of 1995, a 7.2 on the Nojima Fault, images of roads split in two, the city bus hung from a broken highway, the Kashiwai building leaning precariously in one photo, collapsed in the next. It was more difficult for me to see the earthquake that had come and gone in Oakland with the 1918 ordinance introduced in city council to prohibit blacks from buying property in the Santa Fe tract in North

Oakland, with city-wide segregation enforced by vigilante groups, the earthquake that pushed the majority of the city's African American population into West Oakland, where 60% of income in the 1920s and 30s came from service positions with the railroad. The earthquake of segregation that kept coming and going, coming and going with racial covenants and redlining, with state subsidies and New Deal federal housing policies.

And yet during and after the earthquake people always get together. Maybe I imagined the earthquake that is coming because I needed to remember the earthquake that had come and gone. And come again. How people got together during and after, during and after and during. To remember the multi-racial working class neighborhoods of West Oakland in the 1920s and 30s and 40s, the Brotherhood of Sleeping Car Porters, how porters often brought back newspapers to Oakland from Chicago, Los Angeles, even occasionally Atlanta, New Orleans and Birmingham, how information moves around enclosures, sometimes even through them.

But each time the train descended into the tube, as my ears popped as the pressure changed, as I experienced a sense of impending doom or death, rapid heart rate, sweating, shortness of breath, hot flashes, abdominal cramping, chest pain, dizziness, faintness, tightness in my throat, and difficulty swallowing, I felt very alone. The dream of being locked in a nameless room underground. I wanted to imagine people getting together. The multi-racial working class neighborhood. Instead I often found myself imagining the tube cracking, and flooding, and dying down there. In my imagination I always died alone, no matter how many other people might be on the train. There was obviously something wrong with my imagination.

So I struggled to see. How the Key System, a privately owned company that provided mass transit in the East Bay from 1903-1960 and seems to have connected neighborhoods in a far more complex and accessible way, also refused to hire African American workers. Contracted with the U.S. maritime commission to operate the Richmond Shipyard Railway, transporting workers between Oakland, Berkeley, and the shipyards where tens of thousands of mostly African American and women workers were employed during World War I. Where the principal union, the International Brotherhood of Boilermakers, Iron Shipbuilders, and Helpers of America, established segregated locals for African Americans, overseen by white "parent" locals, which kept them powerless, trapped in the tenuous last hired/first fired category.

I kept trying to re-route my imagination but it was slow going, my brain a kind of toddler dazzled and distracted by images of a 7.5 on the Hayward fault. There's no predicting the earthquake, despite videos I sometimes watch in which a man named Luke Thomas narrates a map on the wall, city names and fault zones colored in with sharpie, Luke Thomas runs his finger down the west coast like a weatherman: *risk remains high across the western portion of California, and also the southern. A very dangerous situation.* Situation I longed for and feared in equal measure. Even the symptoms that prevented me from riding BART for so long, and still sometimes propelled my body off the train, especially when crowded with spectators on their way to a sporting event, might indicate profound excitement and anticipation as much as anxiety. Most of the time I travelled by car.

Meanwhile the earthquake that had come and gone kept coming and going, maybe especially wherever people get together, came and went with redevelopment in the 1950s and 60s and 70s, with construction of the Cypress Freeway, the Nimitz, MacArthur and Grove Shafter, the earthquakes that displaced 10,000 people and destroyed between 6,600-9,700 housing units in West Oakland, isolated the neighborhood, walled off the Acorn project and razed the 7th street commercial district.

Came and went with construction of the above-ground portion of the BART line, the Oakland Main Post Office, the Port of Oakland's automated terminal built on landfill and extending into the bay. Came and went with AMCO, with chemicals offloaded and stored in bulk in above ground and underground storage tanks at their storage facility at 1401 Third Street, chemicals that accidentally leaked and were intentionally discarded directly into the soil.

Meanwhile people kept getting together, whenever I imagined the earthquake that is coming I reminded myself of the earthquake that had come and gone. In order to remember the Black Panthers, the main office on Peralta street, Bobby Hutton Park, the free breakfast for school children program, first at St. Augustine's church and later the Intertribal Friendship House. The free clinics, the mobile clinics, the original Clinica de la Raza at Fruitvale and East 15th.

In 1989 a 6.9 earthquake on the San Andreas, its epicenter a full 70 miles away from Oakland, brought down the Cypress Street Viaduct, built on fill. Which is when AMCO chemical closed its distribution center, and community activists fought to keep the Cypress viaduct from being rebuilt in the same location, fought for Mandela Parkway, which wasn't completed until 20 years later and didn't reunite the neighborhood with downtown as promised. Couldn't fix the years and years of earthquakes. Reconstruction took so long. It wasn't until 1996 that CalTrans and PG&E workers were overcome with toxic fumes as they worked on the freeway, which is when leaks at the former AMCO chemical distribution center were discovered, and 1401 Third Street declared a superfund site.

Always the earthquake. Always coming and going. The dredging COINTELPRO Bay Street Emeryville shopping complex container ship superfund asthma cancer earthquake. I could barely even see it most of the time. The earthquake at, and not at, my front door. 434

36th street between Telegraph and Webster. Where I moved back in with Clive. Somewhere between Temescal and Uptown, very near the Santa Fe tract, neighborhoods so often named by developers. Rob Halpern says "Nothing's more real than what we still can't see." I stood in the doorframe of the lower flat, where generally I felt pretty safe. I knew my neighbors and my neighbors knew me. When dogs barked all night or helicopters circled overhead or the police drove through slowly or the police came with their lights flashing, it usually didn't have that much to do with me, by me I guess I meant my skin color, or my job in the bubble, by me I guess I meant my imagination, everything I couldn't see.

It was slow going. The re-routing. I guess I wanted to imagine something that might happen a lot faster. After which people would get together. In a major way. The total transformation of conditions kind of way. There were lots of wrinkles in my idea, Hurricane Katrina for example. People always get together afterwards and the disaster just keeps coming. The disaster has supported support walls. Still, some part of my brain kept stubbornly placing my desire for total transformation alongside my fear of a 7.5 scenario on the Hayward fault, the feeling itself, the ground moving that way, not pretty, not like a train exactly, but some combination of those things. Maybe I wanted to be toppled, I was afraid I'd never fall over on my own, no matter how many credit card bills, thank god for my job in the bubble, every year Clive contracted for less and less, a teaching artist in the schools or leading discussions of the student matinee, no matter how many windows in the lower flat were broken, how high the heating bill, how amazed we were that year to discover mushrooms growing from the kitchen wall, everything really falling apart and yet it was clear we could go on for quite a while this way, the rent so cheap for so much space, so beautiful on a winter afternoon with the red carpets, the light dim. The kettle boiling or soup on the stove. Propped up in bed on two pillows, reading.

I could only seem to imagine myself getting together with other people after hundreds of vehicles are trapped and abandoned along major freeway routes in the East Bay, after half the buildings at the University of California in Berkeley have collapsed or partially collapsed, after 4,000 deaths per 10,000 occupants of unreinforced brick or masonry structures in the high intensity areas.

Everyone is outside in their yards or in the streets. Fires have broken out as a result of broken gas lines. There is no electrical power. Water pressure is nil or rapidly diminishing due to ruptured mains. Traffic signals are inoperative. If it is night, there are no lights, except for flashlights and those of a few vehicles that may be attempting to move. Telephone service is down. Emergency medical aid is unavailable.

I didn't want to be stuck in the tube when it happened. I didn't want to die alone. I didn't want to live alone either, but it was easy to slip into.

BAY OF ANGELS

After New York, after Cincinnati, after I performed the thing I made that failed, and then again after the conferences, after I felt like shit, I kept trying to write through the problem of the person. Rodrigo Toscano says "The person who's striven to cast a light on his or her own culture by way of poetic understanding, by way of searching through the historic density and nested potentials of that person's culture, that person is to be thought of as a treasure map." I felt this way. The problem of the person is a treasure map: I did write this book, I did try hard to write it. Raymond Pettibon says *I Thought California Would Be Different*. I kept attempting to map songlines of persons around me, the mostly leftist poets I am and hang out with. Our songlines so often of reading. Singing of reading, of thinking and writing, of knowledge and scholarship. Singing of professionals and amateurs. Of property and power. Singing with disgust and pleasure, our fingers sometimes caressing one another's faces or pointed towards one another's backs. I wanted to sing with, which sometimes meant singing against.

Sometimes I tried leaving names out. Sometimes I crammed in as many as possible, a return to the slightly hysterical mode of the thing I made that failed. Sometimes I tried writing through figures from other locations and groups and narratives, things far enough away I could play with them as with paper dolls, figures cool enough I could hold in my hands or arrange on a table, the way a child is given toys in a therapist's office. Sometimes I tried to get closer. To this end, I began a project wherein I wrote short histories of books—how they came to be in my possession, where and when I read them, who suggested, loaned or gave the books to me—all the relations that surround reading. I tried not to name titles in this project. I just called them a book, this book. *I don't know how it came to be in my possession: probably this means I bought it.*

The project lasted only briefly, but mapping relations that surround reading became a gesture, a tic I couldn't control. When asked what I was reading, a question posed so often by one poet to another at a party, I found it difficult to answer without also saying that I read this book because of the reading group, because of last July, because he suggested it to me, I'm not sure why, because she so kindly sent it along. I wanted to make so many others visible and audible, wanted to drag up every pressure or gift or fortuitous encounter that helped me think, or hurt, or pushed me over edges into other edges. I didn't mean to presume you are part of me. I didn't mean to presume I am part of you. But secretly, I felt this was true.

I read this book because I was reading many things written by the same group at that time, collectively authored texts on insurrection and alienation that the mostly leftist poets I am and hang out with were also reading. In their short, sometimes beautiful, sometimes ugly, often nonsensical but always very solemn books, this group writes a lot about empire. The call to get organized. Communisation, the sharing of needs. Always alongside a critique of previous movements, a critique of the milieu, a word I could never remember how to pronounce until I split it in two, the *mill you*. And I read this book because you can download it for free as a chapbook from Pétroleuse Press, it prints out double-sided and all that's required is to fold and staple. I printed all the content I could at work without being noticed, on the heels of a free school meeting where we discussed Marxism and feminism, getting them together again. Some people said wait, they were never not together. Others argued the relation felt impoverished in our current moment. How feminism without Marx slides easily into consumerism. Like Nina Power writes: *about as radical as a diamante phone cover*.

In another book by the same group, this argument about an empty feminism of purchasing power gets mapped onto the figure of something called the Young-Girl and ruthlessly critiqued. I'd recently met with some others, poets and artists, to discuss this book. We met in a boutique where the convener of our group worked for wages in a rich neighborhood of San Francisco, "stomping grounds of the Young-Girl herself." The owners gave her access to the boutique after hours for the purpose of this reading group. As the five of us sat on the ground in a circle eating avocados and almonds and bread and apples, the police came by and looked through the window. Shoppers came by and looked through the window. Everyone who looked through the window looked surprised to see us there, sitting on the floor of the boutique after hours. As we sat in a small circle on the floor I railed against the collectively authored, terrifyingly beautiful and repulsive theses, although I had to admit the book's diagnosis of conditions felt devastatingly accurate, in my body: "The Young-Girl is resentment that smiles."

Early on, this book claims the concept of a Young-Girl is not gendered, but rather a figure that reveals how "sociality is now the most precious and prized of commodities," reminding me somewhat painfully of the mostly leftist poets I am and hang out with, how one's status as a writer felt inextricably caught up in social availability and appearance. I mean sexual availability. I mean especially if you were if you are a woman, especially then, if you are a young woman. If you were. And really the text of the book is relentlessly gendered, there is an obsession with her ass, the Young-Girl almost always marked with a feminine pronoun, you can count on your hands the number of times she is referred to as "he," the collective subjectivity so often that of a 15-year-old boy who has been rejected by a girl and wishes to hurt her: "There are certain beings that just make you want to die before their very eyes, but the Young-Girl only excites a desire to conquer and get off on her," how a Marxism or post-Marxism or neo-situationism or insurrectionary anarchism or whatever without feminism can slide easily into sexism, even a hatred of female or feminine bodies. The book does after all come out and say it: that once withdrawn from circulation, I guess that means age, or coupling up, once stripped of her magic aura, "the transcendence that enshrouded her is gone. And she's just a stinking cunt." Is the book *about* the total commodification of female bodies, or is it just misogynist? And shouldn't you be able to tell which it is?

As I am trying to narrate this from the future in such a way that takes into account something I cannot see, I wonder how it was I took this ridiculous writing so seriously—how, on the way to communisation, the sharing of needs, no, on the way to just *reading* about it, I stumbled over this book. It's sort of like the films of Guy Debord, I stumbled over those, too. That diagnosis. Where advertising images of women's bodies stand in for, are, the spectacle over and over again. Cool removed body of the model against a white backdrop, smiling woman in a bikini waist deep in waves, writhing body of the stinking cunt contained in flimsy thong underwear. I stumbled a lot while I tried to stay in the game. The diagnosis so often repeated the conditions. I kept getting caught on identity, constructions, essentially *made-up categories*, as all the leftist poets agreed. Categories that continued to function with ease despite all sorts of diagnosis and critique. Continued to function quite well in the household and pay scale. In the legal system and police force. Such efficiencies radiated outward, or was it inward, touching everything. The mostly leftist poets—I couldn't say they were mostly male, or mostly heteronormative, but sometimes it was easy to feel that way. Power still circulated along those lines. We made jokes about mansplainers and broets. Jokes about social behaviors and subjectivity.

I started reading Bruce Boone because some of the mostly leftist poets I am and hang out with were reading his work at that time. My friends were learning something from Bruce Boone's writing, and I wanted to learn too, which led to sometimes slipping into similar habits of—voice? The book where Bruce Boone is at a Marxist conference and tracing thoughts presented there by Fredric Jameson, "Following Althusser—I think! but I'm no expert here—" When I adopted this tone I tended to sound not so much conversational or intimate with my reader but rather like a young girl. That Boone's book is particularly addressed to some problems of a male and heteronormative Marxism made me want to adopt his tone all the more. I was interested in the way that some mostly male heteronormative poets adopted Bruce Boone's habits of—voice? in part to critique male heteronormativity. I loved this writing. But inhabiting such a voice, sloughing off authority, operated quite differently when the culture accorded one a certain amount of authority to begin with. What did it mean to take up authority? To slough it off? You could see what a relief, how generous it might be. To slough it off. If you had it to begin with. Or I could be dodging something. Hiding out. The old actress isn't good anymore. But she keeps acting. Appearing abject, in order to say something. It depends on how you look at it. From what vantage point.

More than ever I harbored a secret wish to write with mastery, as the narrator in a novel by Roberto Bolaño, *For goodness's sake, Amadeo, I said to myself, you must be drunker than you thought, lost in the fog, with only a little paper lantern hanging from my forward guns, but I didn't panic, and I found the way, step by step, tinkling my little bell, ship on the river, warship lost at the mouth of the river of history, and the honest truth is that by then I was walking as if I were doing that heel-toe dance step, whether it's still something anyone does I don't know, I hope not, touching the heel of the left foot to the toe of the right and then the heel of the right foot to the toe of the left, a ridiculous step but one that had its day, don't ask me when, probably while Miguel Aleman was president, I danced it at some point, we've all done foolish things, and then I heard the door slam and then voices and I said to myself Amadeo stop being an ass and make your way toward the voices, part the mists of this river with your rust-eaten prow and return to your friends, and that's what I did, and I made it to the front room, my arms overflowing with snacks, and the boys were in the front room, sitting there waiting for me, and one of them had bought two bottles of tequila.*

I made my way towards the voices. They were still reading some collectively-authored books by this group, these short, sometimes beautiful, sometimes ugly, often nonsensical but always very solemn books about empire. The call to get organized. Communisation, the sharing of needs. Which is to say insurrectionary texts were somewhat in fashion among the mostly leftist poets I am and hang out with. Maybe because we were interested in collective authorship. In collectivity. I'm not sure if insurrection itself was in style. We kept reading about it, kept talking. Insurrection kept breaking out around us, the world, insurrection was part of *our moment* and we were definitely interested in contemporaneity, in art and writing of its *moment*.

One day I managed to arrive somewhat absentmindedly at this book. I pulled it out from the stack of collectively authored texts by Tiqqun, the same group who wrote *Raw Materials for a Theory of the Young-Girl*. Picked it up with curiosity, partly because the word *community* appears in its title, and partly because the word *terrible* modifies *community*. This combination felt related to all the problems I was snagged on, all the shit on my mind, and while there are obviously many other books I might have picked up, recently fashionable books with *community* in the title, I didn't. Didn't arrive somewhat absentmindedly at *The Unavowable Community* or *Inoperative Community* or *The Coming Community* or *Communitas: The Origin and Destiny of Community*. I could have picked up a book a little less insurrectionary. But I made my way by making my way towards the voices. For a moment these were the books they spoke of. I made my way towards them. I arrived somewhat absentmindedly, in that fashion.

Later, I would find a way to arrive at this writing less absentmindedly, would write in the *Poetry Project Newsletter* that "Probably any number of factors make Tiqqun interesting to U.S. poets, from general interest in all things continental theory to the shift in weather following 2008's economic crisis. There's the writing itself, which even Wikipedia notes is poetic. Also plenty of heroic glamour. Giorgio Agamben wrote a public editorial in defense of Julien Coupat, the journal's co-founder, after his 2008 arrest and charges under France's anti-terrorism laws for disrupting train service. Other public support includes a petition published in *Le Monde* and signed by luminaries such as Alain Badiou, Judith Butler, and Zlavoj Zizek. The case against Coupat included alleged authorship of *The Coming Insurrection*, a book much reviled by Glenn Beck. Not since Ginsberg's obscenity trial have the stakes of a book of been so high. It's possible poets and artists are more interested in Tiqqun's writing (and take it more seriously) than political theorists and activists. Responses to their work at anarchist news dot org tend towards the critical, such as Anon's dismissive post on *This is Not A Program*: "Once again saying they are the opposite of things in italics, once again rupturing with things, once again universalizing bourgeois French intellectualism…Again all this: sex, action, excitement, big words, petty leftist squabbling (and it's new!)." You can see why poets might love it. The distribution model feels familiar too; multiple free PDFs circulate online, often followed by official publication in semiotext(e)'s intervention series."

You can see why I might have taken this writing so seriously in the past, how it was I could arrive somewhat absentmindedly, in that fashion, might stumble but also feel implicated again, diagnosed, which the book did after all warn me of: *Watch out! A dangerous chapter to read because everybody is challenged*. The networks, the platforms, the conferences and anxiety about conferences, the antagonism between workers inside and outside the academy, the constant questioning of the group and its politics, who and what is visible there, all this I found reflected in the collectively authored *Theses on the Terrible Community*: "The less a community feels the sensation of its existence, the more it is compelled to externally actualize its own enactment, in activism, in compulsive gathering and finally in the constant metastatic questioning of itself. The never ending collective self-criticism that the management of avant-garde groups more and more visibly engages in, as well as the informal groups of neo-militants, rather demonstrates the decisive weakness in their sentiment that they exist."

What was my hysterical mode of naming names if not a demonstration of the decisive weakness in my sentiment that the community existed, that I existed within it?

What is this failure I'm writing, if not that which partakes of the never-ending self-criticism that the management of avant-garde groups more and more visibly engages in?

Implicated in my reading, lost in the fog, with only a little paper lantern hanging from my forward guns, I felt diagnosed. But also something very like grief, as I read this book and others that surrounded it, reading that surrounded friendships with the mostly leftist poets I am and hang out with, as we thought more and more about radical history and social movements. Labor. Resistance. Solidarity. Especially as I read *Caliban and the Witch*, which so many poets were also reading at that time, I felt my failure diagnosed from the past, missing information flooded in, something very like grief, as if for the dead, my own, persons I'd loved for a moment and lost, how "we can imagine what effect it had on women to see their neighbors, friends and relatives being burned," midwives become spies for the state, communal lands fenced off, the body taken from itself, its labor obscured, that which the body had done for love, or if not for love at least for others it could see and touch—monetized. The spike driven between us so long ago, burned to death for our alliances, riots at the enclosures in groups of 37 and 47 and 15, women digging up the hedges, yet relentlessly "polarized not only by the deepening economic inequalities, but by a web of hatred and resentments that is well-documented in the records of the witch-hunt, which show that quarrels relating to requests for help, the trespassing of animals, or unpaid rents were in the background of many accusations."

The choke of competition.

Was that it? I felt like we were facing each other from the edges of a very dark and scary crater. Truth and difficulty. Truth and sex. I was talking, you were listening.

In the first section of the thing I made that failed, immediately following the sound that nobody recognized, the sounds that came before, and the sounds that came after the shot that killed Oscar Grant, the brief but total silence surrounding the shot, immediately after these sounds play on a loop in the dark, we see Jeanne Moreau and Claude Mann in a hotel room in Nice. They're down on their luck but they still look good. They're getting dressed to go out. To dinner, to the casinos. They've obviously just had sex before this scene begins, although we don't see that. Moreau turns towards the camera with a white feather boa. Sits at a vanity applying makeup. Describes some facts about the construction of BART. Moreau in the mirror, her eyes are big. The scene is from *Bay of Angels*. Netflix says *Love is a gamble in this 1963 film directed by Jacques Demy.*

It's a commonplace that participants at all sorts of conferences often sleep together in the bad hotels where such conferences are held. A commonplace that such sex, in bad hotels at conferences, is banal, or bourgeois, empty—helplessly entangled in the abjection of work for wages. Generally the figure associated with such sex is a salesperson. I'm thinking of the conference scene from that that movie *Up in the Air*. People in suits at a bar. George Clooney. The first section of the thing I made that failed isn't about sex at conferences, although I do mention the MLA Offsite Reading as yet another location where Jeanne Moreau has spoken neurotically about her fear of riding BART. *God, you can't stop talking about it, can you!* Seconds later, Claude Mann slaps her, is immediately contrite, *I'm sorry, darling, you don't ever have to ride BART again...I'm so sorry...*

Moreau terrifies me in this movie, with her bleached blonde hair and aging face, she's so obviously desperate, so obviously the other side of that sexist song by the Stranglers, *So Nice in Nice*: Just look at that girl / She walks around owning everything / That's not even hers / She's got diamond rings from her dad / She's got fancy things from her dad / All the world wants my baby / All the world wants her.

So nice in nice.

I didn't feel very nice. I was a terrible community. Plus I was getting old. A stinking cunt. Still thinking about the conference. The teeth. The tape. How the academic poetics conference had come to loom very large in a series of overlapping local poetry networks that comprised a loose national scene, come to loom very large in the imagination of the mostly leftist poets I am and hang out with, larger than academic conferences generally do, which is usually not at all. Or only very barely, and then only when they serve as an occasion of sociality. Such as when the MLA was held in San Francisco a few years ago.

At the ritual MLA Offsite Reading, occasioned each year in a different city by the visit of so many out of town poets, but featuring roughly equal numbers of local poets and out of town poets who either have or are trying to obtain a job in the academy, the poets all the poets generally seem happy to be together in their shared revulsion of the MLA, in so much as it represents the abjection of having and seeking jobs. To interview in a hotel room. To work for wages. Somehow it's easy for the poets all the poets to hate on the MLA together, or at least be somewhat dismissive of the MLA together, or treat the MLA as the unfortunate requirement that occasions this other pleasure, of so many poets hanging out together in a place and time they would not otherwise. And yet the pleasure is all mixed up in the abjection, the competition for a dwindling handful of tenure line academic positions.

At the MLA, at the AWP, it all gets conflated: the sex, the tables, the gambling, the abjection of work for wages.

This seemed both true and not true in the local poetry community. The mostly leftist poets I am and hang out with felt, wanted to feel, *otherwise*, that the entanglement of our bodies as we folded and stapled chapbooks and talked on the phone, as we made out in pairs and groups and met on the platform, as we rehearsed and set up chairs and took them down again, as we donated money to the small press through paypal and fucked, that all this might be outside, or at least somewhat to the side of, somewhat less helplessly entangled in the tables, the gambling, the wages. That our love might be something other than, or opposite the Young-Girl's *autism for two*. Might be emancipatory, and radical.

I felt this way, I did write this book, I did try hard to write it.

But so often, the mostly leftist poets I am and hang out with seemed unable to feel or do *otherwise*—as we folded and stapled chapbooks we were often lying to our girlfriend or boyfriend as we made out in pairs and groups and talked on the phone, as we told her "I don't want to be in a relationship with Kathy Acker," as we met on the platform and said with a wink that lots of men in the Department would be *very happy* if she entered the PhD program, as we rehearsed and set up chairs we were often publishing mostly white men in our project and then getting defensive when someone pointed it out, as we took the chairs down again and slept with our friend's husband while she was out of town, as we donated money to the small press through paypal and fucked our students, as we casually sexualized young female poets in conversation we were often aggressively pursuing them at readings, pressuring them with our sexual attention such that many felt uncomfortable and some stopped attending readings altogether, as we watched our friends became *that guy*.

So often we repeated the conditions. That women's bodies have been the main targets. In history that has happened yes. Privileged sites for the deployment of power techniques. Power-relations.

In this and so many other ways, the mostly leftist poets I am and hang out with countered ourselves getting together. With each other but others too. Possible allies. Alliances we might have made. So often we repeated the conditions. We kept getting caught on identity, constructions, essentially *made-up categories*, as all the leftist poets agreed. Categories like gender that continued to function with ease despite all sorts of diagnosis and critique. Continued to function quite well in the household and pay scale. In the legal system and police force. Such efficiencies radiated outward, or was it inward, touching everything. The reading series and publishing project too. So often we stumbled and tripped, caught as we were in fragmentation of the public sphere and sexual division of labor, we acted out in the uneven distribution of resources and ordinary daily violence of love, illness, labor, birth, rape, fractured by structural contradictions and imposition of beauty as a condition for social acceptability, divided by legacies of prior organization and political conflict, dominated by elite interests. Our interdependencies of work, consumption, and residence, our voluntary associations of folding and stapling and fucking, our networks of mutual dependency and support—all still harbored exclusionary and hierarchical relations of private power. Even as we felt, wanted to feel, *otherwise*.

Polarized not only by the deepening economic inequalities, but by a web of hatred and resentments, in the background of our accusations.

We were depressed and anxious. Diagnosed with panic disorder. Dissociated during sex.

Depressed, and deeply paranoid. We surveilled one other on the privately owned networks that collected our keystrokes and search terms, monitored our habits of consumption, and those of our lovers and friends.

The terrible community is a sum of solitudes that, without protecting itself, keeps itself under surveillance.

So often we said nothing when he called her trashy or dominated the conversation or lied to his girlfriend or dismissed her as not very smart. We cringed and winced at the casually ironic racism in her poem. We complained in private but continued to attend the series that presented mostly white male writers. We heard that he hit or slapped his girlfriend but performed at the event anyways. We laughed uncomfortably as he said with a wink that lots of men in the department would be *very happy* if she entered the PhD program. Is the joke about misogyny, or is it just misogynist? And shouldn't you be able to tell which it is?

Mark Wallace says "One of the reasons that poets love Roberto Bolaño's novels is that he puts poets at the center of the world he describes, and involves them in intellectual, sexual, and political struggles with significant, and often socially large scale, consequences."

Bifo says, "As a general tendency, work is performed according to the same physical patterns: we all sit in front of a screen and move our fingers across a keyboard. We type."

I got so angry when I first read that. It's from *The Soul at Work*. I read this book because, as I surveilled my friends on the internet, I noticed several of them were reading it. I got so angry at the we of this book, composed of certain workers of a certain class, a we that excluded so many others whose work was not performed according to the same physical patterns as the mostly leftist poets I am and hang out with. Workers who do not, as a general tendency, type. Workers who might instead work for 3 days straight, 12 hours a day, to produce the first generation of Apple's iPad, or live in a shack built from recycled garage doors in a neighborhood with no sewage lines or electricity, or suffer from kidney damage and lead poisoning from years of exposure to toxic chemicals, or drown in the flooding of a goldmine in Nicaragua owned by B2Gold Corp in Canada, or be forced to take pregnancy tests, or arrested, detained, tortured and killed for organizing workers in Bangladesh's apparel industry.

If this were a scene from a movie, a self-involved movie, I would have thrown this book across the room. Instead I set it down with a sigh. Secretly I was angry with my friends about the we of this book and even in some way held them accountable for it. My anger was irrational and unfair. I didn't even know why several friends were reading this book, or what they thought of it—surveillance only goes so far. I only knew the book had moved among them with great speed and quotation on the internet. My friends found something meaningful about this book: what?

What did my friends want? In this movie I play the lover, and my friends the ever-elusive beloved, or I am the parent trying to understand my alienated teenager, or the wife who hires a private detective to follow her increasingly distant husband. Polarized not only by the deepening economic inequalities, but by a web of hatred and resentments, in the background of my private accusations. But I did think this book, this we, was connected to the overall privilege of myself and everyone I couldn't stop addressing in the thing I made that failed, and everything I wrote afterwards, connected to the overall privilege of the mostly leftist poets I am and hang out with.

Months later I picked this book up again. And saw that Bifo does briefly account for workers who do not type, for uneven distribution of resources and internal stratification. Accounts especially for technological transitions, the internet that makes certain kinds of organizing and disruptive communities harder and harder to build. He diagnoses some conditions. I started to think that maybe I needed this book to help decipher some bad feelings around the networked platforms where I met and meet my friends, some login pages, some linking strategies, "a pathogenic separation between cognitive functions and material sociality." Started to think that maybe I needed the community poetics and labor conference to understand the conditions, the structures, antagonisms that made getting together so complicated. Maybe I needed *Raw Materials for a Theory of the Young-Girl* to understand just how deeply the revulsion runs.

Maybe I got so angry with Bifo, with my friends, with Tiqqun, because I just keep reading and nothing changes. Because the diagnosis so often repeats the conditions.

Maybe I got so angry with Bifo because I keep failing in the same way, not differently or better. I just keep typing. Addressing myself to the mostly leftist poets I am and hang out with. A small group of people in a local. Repeating those conditions. I keep getting stuck in something that is not exactly involvement in struggles with socially large consequences. I keep reading insurrectionary texts and talking about them. I keep standing by silently while he says with a wink that lots of men in the department would be *very happy* if she entered the PhD program. I keep cringing at the casually ironic racism of her poem. I keep making a face, complaining in private. I keep making jokes about mansplainers.

Maybe I got so angry because secretly, stubbornly, and in exhaustion, I couldn't see any other way to proceed, to fail until something changed. To just keep reading. Keep typing. Address myself to those who read, address myself to those who type.

Is that even true? What was I, who were you, the mostly leftist poets I am and hang out with? In our status as receptionists, salespeople for drug companies, executive assistants, unemployed, administrators of all kinds, ghostwriters for fundraisers, fundraisers for non profits, parents, graduate students, literacy advocates, psychoanalytic psychotherapists, booksellers, coordinators, program directors, programmers, more or less substantial English professors—it couldn't even be said that we all typed. We couldn't be said to comprise a class when the ties that bound us were something else, something done for free, but increasingly and uncomfortably entangled in the abjection of work for wages, the astonishing growth in MFA programs and degree holders of all kinds.

Nor could it be said we were all leftist, or middle class, or white. It depends on how you look at it. From what vantage point. Who do I leave out when I say mostly white? Mostly middle class? Mostly leftist? I notice I never say mostly male, or mostly heteronormative. Because I know who that would leave out. I notice I'm fairly good at not leaving myself out, although often afraid that others will.

Did we constitute a kind of family? A "speculative mutuality"? The "cognitariat"? We were not a church, not a union, not a neighborhood association, not an advocacy group, although at moments we partook of these things. I thought for a second that we came closest to being the spontaneous conviviality of the daily round, but that wasn't quite right either. We were an abstraction. Deeply divided. Striated. But also a temporal thickness of shared activities.

The more I typed, the tighter the teeth of the ratchet on the tape, the way through the problem, the sound nobody recognized, the thing I made that failed. Couldn't be separated from other failures. We countered ourselves getting together. With each other but others too. Possible allies. Alliances we might have made, but didn't.

I still didn't know how to talk about it.

Maybe, at our best, and worst, we were a reading group. Down on our luck but we still looked good. We were getting dressed to go out. To dinner, to the casinos. Reading insurrectionary texts and talking about them. Interested in collectivity, in Marxism and feminism, getting them together again.

Moreau turns towards the camera with a white feather boa. She sits at a vanity applying makeup. Describes some facts about the construction of BART. Moreau in the mirror, her eyes are big. The scene is from *Bay of Angels*.

IN WHICH METAPHORS FOR POETRY COMMUNTIES, AND FOR WRITING ABOUT THEM, ABOUND

(posted April 3, 2011, *http://jacket2.org/commentary/which-metaphors-poetry-communties-and-writing-about-them-abound*)

I'm hopelessly devoted to the downtown Oakland YMCA, with spin classes spinning next to morning tai chi, basketball games in the gym followed by African dance class. I love the late afternoon afterschool program sounds, double dutch in the mind-body studio. There's free childcare, coffee in the lobby, wheelchairs, a mentoring program, book exchange, elevators, and financial aid. It's basically sliding scale, a utopia. Its members are multi-ethnic and multi-lingual, like the city it is part of. Bodies at the Oakland Y tend not to be all that beefcake, nor all that svelte. Or, there are as many bodies as there are genders and generations. In a culture that is so persistently fucked up around bodies, being in the locker room at the downtown Oakland YMCA feels like some kind of psychic survival tactic, being with so many other naked sweaty bodies, not images, blemished and muscular and round, people icing their knees, rubbing oils into the skin, blow drying their hair, not blow drying their hair, having conversations. It's not a space where anyone can be only with others who are like themselves. I want to say it's one of the only spaces like this in the city where I live, but that's just an idea, anecdotal, probably my blind spots talking.

If Bay Area poetry communities were mapped onto a building, it would look very different from the downtown Oakland YMCA. There would be one ramshackle addition after another built off the back, private rooms requiring arcane passwords, some tents in the parking lot, a bank of classrooms by the locker rooms, actually I do not think there would be locker rooms, sadly, at least not a women's locker room, but there would be roving one-person galleries, workshops, potlucks, stacks and stacks of chapbooks, lecture halls and theaters, reading groups, a BYOB bar, doors that don't work. Access to one part of the building wouldn't guarantee access to another. You could be spinning next door to a tai chi class and never even know it. Which is to say it's totally possible, for example, to see Judy Grahn read at Moe's Books one month, and then Steve Farmer and Ron Silliman in that same space the next, with little to no overlap in audience. (Something I will be doing soon, and reporting on here. UPDATE: due to scheduling vagaries I missed the latter, alas, but you can find Robin Tremblay-McGaw's excellent report here, and I'll be typing up my notes on the Grahn reading soon.) The Bay Area is probably not all that unique in this respect. The Bowery Poetry Club in New York comes to mind as a particular example of very different programming and communities existing in the same building, one group leaving as "their" reading ends, another streaming in. And I am of course not at all unique in trying to think about these things—while writing this post I've been reading Sarah Rosenthal's book of interviews with Bay Area writers, *A Community Writing Itself*, where Robert Glück says many smart and tender things about writing communities in the Bay Area. And he talks about the 1981 Small Press Traffic conference he organized, *Left/Write*, which "brought together writers who were famous in their own scene and hardly known beyond it—like Judy Grahn and Ron Silliman speaking on the same panel." 1981.

The YMCA is perhaps not the best metaphor in the world for what I'm trying to think about, or at least a complicated one, given that organization's history as a christian non-profit. Its political commitments might as well be the pursuit of happiness. And yet it seems remarkably successful at doing some things the local poetry communities I hang out in seem unable to do, despite talking and thinking together all the time about radical change and social transformation.

One of the things I am trying to think about, or through, is James Edward Smethurst's excellent book on the Black Arts Movement which traces conditions and relations out of which that movement emerged, including popular front aesthetics, old left connections, and what Smethurst calls a multi-racial bohemian scene, especially that of the Lower East Side, but also North Beach. (And it's interesting to see how east/west coast differences show up, including a separatist impulse in the Bay Area inflected by geography, for instance: Bolinas.) Smethurst also traces relationships between the New American Poetry and the Black Arts Movement (and Chicana/o and Asian American writers), relationships between people but also between institutions and publications. Reading this book is renovating, once again, the part of my brain that received a friendship such as Baraka and O'Hara's as individual, or exceptional. It's the same part of my brain that is trying to think about this Jeffrey Joe Nelson poem:

> 2. 11. 2011
>
> In Tahir Square in Cairo
> & In Steinway Street in Queens
> & In the streets of Quetta, Bahrain,
> Lebanon, Palestine, Tunisia, Algeria,
> Iran, Sudan, Yemen, Jordan & Libya
> the people are raising their shoes,
> raising their voices, raising their fingers
> to point at their leaders, asking them
> why, why, why, in America, in Queens
> why, Brikily, in dark rooms lit by computer
> screens some of us ask why, as well
> but not nearly enough of us
> not nearly fucking
> enough!
> . . .
>
>   jeffrey joe nelson

So many parts of my brain need to be renovated again and again. Jessica Lowenthal's invitation to write "about and around Bay poetics" for the next few months has prompted something of a crisis in renovation, especially my received ideas about community formations, schools and movements, and how the construction of these things inflect any view of the present, a view which can only ever be incomplete. Something of a crisis about what it means to do documentary writing around Bay Area poetry communities, around poets and reading series and presses, poems and performances and chapbooks.

Thus I've been wandering the back corridors as *Jacket2* prepares to launch, talking to myself. It's not unlike hanging out in a theater during tech week. People are warming up, embedding videos and sound files, doing their scales, playing around with the sidebar. It's exciting. At first I'd turn down a hallway and see a block of latin placeholder text, but now every day I bump into a new review or article. I'm feeling very wow to be in such great company, very wow about a clear editorial intention to bring many different writers into the building, to think about many different kinds of poetry.

As I've thought about how to approach this commentary writing, which might have felt simple ten years ago and not so simple now, I've also been thinking about the important role *Jacket* (the first) and other online locations played in my early education as a poet, in mapping out scenes of contemporary poetry. Institutions played their part in this mapping, but looking at the internet and reading the journals and books I read about there, on listserv discussions and then blogs, was in many ways more helpful. In figuring out where I might fit as a writer. In the pre-facebook early aughts, it was still a national/transnational internet that helped me find my way into a local poetry community, one that's wound up meaning an awful lot to me. Which is to say I sort of backed my way into the local room by way of figuring out a mostly national scene of experimental/postmodern/avant-garde/innovative writing. As I backed my way into the room, I carried in all my received ideas and inherited maps. The maps were useful, they helped me find my friends and comrades, but they also told partial stories, as all maps do, were missing important information. Which meant for a long time I only saw a few rooms of the building, or only heard a few of the stories that got told about a room's history. This seems like a not uncommon experience, I'm thinking here of my friend who found his way to his contemporaries by way of following the bio notes and publications listed in *In The American Tree*. Which was a great way in, one way in. You start with a map that's meaningful, and feel your way into the present. Then it opens up. The maps keep moving. You have to keep renovating your brain.

Bay Poetics is an anthology I edited in 2005. In retrospect, editing an anthology seems like a slightly insane thing to have done. I'm not sure what sense of permission allowed me to wade into the troubled waters of map making in the first place. Without a co-editor, even. Some kind of total joyful ignorance. As I worked on the anthology, the overwhelming complication of attempting such a project came into view. After the anthology came out I fielded a lot of questions about what might be particular to contemporary Bay Area poetry as constructed in the anthology, what aesthetic or formal impulses poems in the book might share, and I always found a way to dodge these. It seemed dumb, and impossible, to make regional claims about one's current moment, especially when all I could see were my blind spots, the gaps, writers who weren't included.

This was perhaps one way to avoid thinking about whatever it was I *had* made; how my editorial practice in Bay Poetics at moments inherited, and at other moments resisted, the logic of earlier maps and anthologies, exclusionary frameworks, contested histories, community institutions, MFA programs. It's definitely a big book, with writing from 112 people. With this bigness I wanted to something about the way maps don't hold, or are always drawn in the service of power, the way they gloss things, and must be re-thought at every turn. But in retrospect, *Bay Poetics* was too big to make a claim about anything other than the uselessness of map making (along with a comment on the proliferation of people writing and publishing poetry, and maybe also a comment on the proliferation of MFA programs.) Its size made certain things, like specificity, impossible. But neither was it comprehensive. It wasn't nearly as large as it might have been. It didn't venture beyond one or two rooms.

Lately I wonder how *Bay Poetics* might have been both more specific than it was, and larger than it was. Is there a way to do both. Is there a way to do that here.

Often I dodged the questions about regional specificity by talking about my obsession with social relations as embedded in the anthology, embodied in the book's ordering. How sex might have as significant an impact on the formation and reformation of poetry communities as educational and community institutions. I want to say that this obsession with social relations might in fact be one shared concern in the local experimental/postmodern/avant-garde/innovative poetry community I mostly hang out in. Maybe I will start calling this local scene "my neck of the woods." Where there's a keen interest in sociality, exchange, power relations, group formations, the local's interest in the local as such, the local talking to itself, basically, although a local that can include, at moments, individuals in Cincinnati and Brooklyn, Buffalo or Detroit. Perhaps that's overstated. But experimental/postmodern/avant-garde/innovative poetry communities in the Bay Area are, after all, deeply informed by Jack Spicer, whose relationship to locality verged on the religious, by the primacy of gossip and liberatory sexual politics in New Narrative writing, by the project of *The Grand Piano* and the histories of collaboration it writes through, by the fallout of the poetry wars, the tensions and turf skirmishes from the last moment in which Bay Area poetry communities might have understood themselves to even be occupying a common building. (Shampoo Poetry's calendar of Bay Area Poetry Events might come closest to suggesting this might still be the case in some way.)

Kaplan Harris keeps usefully complicating my sense of these overlapping influences in his recent papers "Causes, Movements, Poets" and "The Small Press Traffic School of Dissimulation," both of which re-think maps and movements, received notions of conflict and division, often highlighting instead the uneasy and unexpected alliances within the experimental/postmodern/avant-garde/innovative tradition, including shared moments of activism and resistance, moments of "terrific argument" around aesthetics and political life. I'm interested in those moments, moments that weren't a part of the maps I inherited. I'm not sure if that's about the maps, or the way I read them, what I did and didn't look at when I was looking my way in. I think and talk a lot about what's changed since then. What might keep such moments from happening now. How perhaps more communication and alliance between parts of the building might be necessary if such moments are ever going to emerge again, however differently they might appear, in Bay Area poetry communities. What would that even look like. What terrific argument.

So while I'll be reporting on my neck of the woods while I'm here, I'm also giving myself the assignment to check out other parts of the Bay Area, other scenes. There are many individuals who do this, show up in more than one place, and their movement helps trace the persistent bridges and tunnels between rooms. I'd like to understand more about those connections. Because if Bay Area poetry communities were the downtown Oakland YMCA, I've been doing pretty much exactly what I do at the downtown Oakland YMCA, 30 minutes on the elliptical machine by the window a few times a week, followed by some stretching and 10 minutes in the sauna. Sometimes a yoga class, but mostly that same deal on the elliptical machine. This is a great routine and helps with my generalized anxiety, but also it is never going to change my body in any radical way, it is pretty comfortable.

I almost just launched another metaphor here, about cross-training, but stopped myself.

Maybe it is simpler than I think, or, this sentence from the *The Coming Insurrection*: "The rule is simple: the more territories there are superimposed on a given zone, the more circulation there is between them, the harder it will be for power to get a handle on them." Like Love & Rockets, No New Tale To Tell. So I will look at very small things with my eyes. I will go to some events and listen. There will be some blurry photographs. I will say some things. In the internet of the Bay Area of one person's reporting I will probably get some things wrong. Whenever I can, I'll veer into the (my) blind spots. "We'll see."

THE FAST

I read this book because Alli lent it to me. She said it was the kind of book you could read very quickly, which is almost exactly what I said when I told her that same evening about Nina Power's *One Dimensional Woman*, a book I borrowed from Juliana. Both are around 50 pages.

As I went through my bag one morning, trying to figure out how to proceed in writing through the thing I made that failed, I held the book in my hands and looked at its cover. In the lower left hand corner there is a black and white drawing of a woman's legs, she is lying on a blanket or a sheet and two beautiful tigers spring from her foot. Tucked between the book's pages, I found some photographs from Alli, prints from her flickr page, which I placed on the mantle next to a card from Thessaly, a beautiful wise and eerie owl on a deep, green-blue background as deep and dimensional as brocade.

I didn't read the book all at once but I did read it in a few days. It was a lot to take in. I don't know how not to say this book is by Hannah Weiner. In it she describes a fast of around 3 weeks. It is a book of colors and energies, of visions, becoming sight and hearing, perhaps of going mad, of living in an apartment where there are rats, how wage labor shows up in the hands, how living in a city shows up in the back and legs, a book of becoming allergic, or the word Weiner uses, *magnetic*, to metals and electricity. It is a book about not having a bathtub during a time of extremity and physical tension and transformation. I had a hard time the two years I lived without a bathtub. Sometimes getting in the water is the only thing that helps.

I felt somewhat dim while reading this book, in which Weiner becomes so sensitive to the energy of her own body and others and enters into a kind of severe housecleaning, washing away the purple and green which cause pain, how she can feel when a yellow or red person passes by the door to her studio, how she is calling out for a blue to help her at the end. I can't see any colors. The closest thing I can think of is the hottest pool at the hot springs, between 112-15 degrees, and all the anger that rushes up my spine every time I enter the hottest pool for the first time. It is the worst if someone is waiting behind you to go down the stairs, someone who's just come from the cold pool and can move easily and quickly into the hot, can slip right in. After you go into the cold you understand they are the same. But the first time into the hottest pool I have to endure all the irritation and anger that goes rushing up my spine. And the first time into the cold, the awful feelings of loss, as blood rushes out of my fingers and toes, towards the interior.

Every time I go into the hottest pool for the first time I can only make it down the stairs and then lean against the wall that separates it from the warm pool. There is a little hole in the wall where water flows out. It's not any cooler there, but I like knowing I'm near a cooler space, like poking holes in a yam before you bake it. It's impossible to move any further into the hottest pool the first time in, impossible to move nearer the mouth of the dolphin or maybe it's a whale, whose mouth the hot water pours from, and which people sometimes stand under, water pouring over their heads and shoulders, incomprehensible as I stand against the wall between things. Later, after the cold, standing under the water's mouth makes more sense although it's still not for me. I like to rest my head on a wooden bench on either side of the dolphin's mouth. Sinuous metal bars run above the benches and with a small hop you can reach up and grab on, swing yourself out of the water, and when you get it right, it's perfect, your feet land in a crouch on the bench, or your ass slides up and the legs and feet follow, and I think that might be how it felt when Hannah Weiner was half asleep in the sink and awoke mid-leap, landing on her good foot.

Every time I go into the hottest pool for the first time, I stand against the wall and suffer as people glide by and move up and down the stairs, because every time a person moves, they cause waves of hot water to push against my body and then irritation and anger all along the spine. Whenever this happens I am reminded that water only conducts energy from other bodies, and this must be happening all the time in the air, and I just can't pick up on it, these waves which become beautiful and various after you've gone back and forth between the hottest and cold pool a few times, which is why everyone should observe the SILENCE rule because if someone talks or does that weird performative moaning you hear too often there, it is agony. There are already so many waves going on. This experience is part of why I feel dull reading Hannah Weiner, because I can only pick up energy from other bodies when it is being conducted through 112-15 degree water. And even then I can't see any colors.

This experience of the hot pool is also what makes me sympathetic to the book. And the book makes me sympathetic towards my predicament. Maybe what I was trying to do, in the thing I made that failed, and everything I kept making afterwards that kept doing the same thing, was partly about the red and green and purple energies. The energy inside my body, and the energy coming from other bodies. Weiner spends a lot of the book trying to deal with purple coming from her own body that causes so much pain. I wondered if the pain I so often experienced around the poets I am and hang out with was a purple. My own.

I started to think that maybe I didn't need to worry so much about whether the pain was coming from my own body or others, individuals or a group, that the colors I couldn't see but only feel could be coming from my own body and also the bodies of others at the same time. And obviously the painful colors had something or everything to do with fragmentation of the public sphere and sexual division of labor, with uneven distribution of resources and the ordinary daily violence of love, illness, labor, birth, rape—with exclusionary and hierarchical relations of private power.

The book had me starting to think differently about all the things I'd written after I made the thing that failed, and how they all felt like a version of the same thing, over and over, and that maybe this was ok, like how Weiner had to clean the purple from her body over and over. How she had to be careful because if she worked too long cleaning one area, like her shin, the pain would just move into the knee, her bad knee. How she had to work slowly and with great care to release the pain and not just move it to another part of the body. Pouring little cups of water over different parts while sitting in the sink, since she didn't have a bathtub, rubbing her back with a wooden spoon, how all her clothes got contaminated with the purple, even the little glasses could only be re-used so many times before they too became all colored with the purple and had to be thrown in a pile with the rest, the favorite blankets and sweaters all had to be thrown away. How wrapping her feet in yellow notepad paper was the only way to move from place to place in the studio.

But also I felt some dread while reading this book because Paul told me earlier in the year that I tended to think in metaphors but this wasn't one, the experience of my body wasn't a metaphor. He told me this during the same session in which he described the book I would write, it would be called *URSULA or UNIVERSITY*. Ursula is a female witch who steals the voices of others and/or turns them into statues. University is sort of where I work. Paul said the cover of the book would be purple.

As I write this I am trying to drown out the sound of my neighbor's voice from the house next door. Shouting. Drowning out the sound of the place where I live in order to write something. Even as the energy of the place where I live is part of my body and entering it. And this is probably a large part of why the thing I made that failed, failed.

As I write this I'm looking out the window of a high bourgeois café at a dog waiting expectantly for his owner. When I look up again, that dog's gone and another one's taken his place. There's an endless procession of dogs who wait outside.

I was a dog who wanted other dogs. I was a dog and other dogs could be in my place.

I had to stop thinking in metaphors.

SUMMER 2011

In the summer of 2011, in the area, the Bay Area, some of my friends were learning Spanish. Some were learning Greek, some were learning Latin, some I think were learning Arabic and eating breakfast together every Sunday morning. Some were traveling. Some were meeting to read *Alma*. Some were meeting to read *Capital*. Some were performing a marathon reading of Gertrude Stein's work at SFMoma to celebrate an exhibition of artworks collected by the Stein family. Some were talking about organizing events at La Pena Cultural Center, in the hopes of making some connections between some poets and some other poets. Some were drinking rosé and swimming in a river. Some were going on the Black Panther tour and talking with David Hilliard. Some were raising little babies and toddlers and adolescents. Some were ill or dying. Some were recovering. Most were working during the day, the evening, and on weekends. Some were overemployed, some were underemployed, and some were unemployed.

Some were writing this at an artist residency, eating rich and sustainable foods, making friends with composers from Mexico City and poets from Morocco and artists from Los Angeles and Arizona, and walking through the surrounding neighborhoods of empty and enormous houses with vineyards for lawns, the streets empty save for gardeners who tended the lawns and vineyards of these empty houses. I kept joking that this was the most violent neighborhood I'd ever lived in.

Some were working on the Poetic Labor Project, an outgrowth of the community poetics and labor conference. Every month my friends the organizers posted writing online from various writers and locations including many who worked in the academy. *Anne Boyer is a single mother who works three jobs in the ivory basement, or for at least two of these jobs, the sub-sub ivory basement.* I felt grateful for this project if also small-minded, *trifling*, as I continued to type about the conference of the year before. Worse than small minded. As I typed I got sweaty, anxious. I'd sit at the keyboard, hands to my head, what was I doing? I was a leaky mistress. A gigantic baby. I was afraid of getting in trouble. Or causing trouble. Which is it? I felt like we were facing each other from the edges of a very dark and scary crater.

Meanwhile some of my friends were attending a conference on anarchy at the New School. This conference didn't have anything to do with poetry, didn't really register among the mostly poets I am and hang out with. I watched as it registered among anarchists. It sounded familiar. One post described the conference on anarchy as "all-too-academic," and another blogger complained that it was "…slightly behind the times. Consider that in 2005 David Graeber shouted 'Hello we exist' in an effort to awaken the dead in the corridors of contemporary universities."

I kept seeing similarities between the radical and anarchist communities I was learning about, and the mostly poets I am and hang out with. Each with specialized knowledge and vocabulary, each with crippling internal disagreements and fighting. Each with some divisions around the academy. Each staunchly anti-sexist and anti-racist, and yet with some problems around sexism, mostly white or seeming to be. And yet each with long, rich histories of women doing and leading, of multi-racial organizing and milieus. Neither seemed like something one would really want to tell a stranger seated next to you on a plane, if asked what kind of writing you do, what sort of politics. Although at least one of the friends I love does in fact answer when asked on a plane, hopes to be asked, so he can say he is a poet. What does he write about? The usual things: sex, love, and death.

When my friend returned from the conference, she told me about a talk she heard there. I watched it by myself, at the artist residency, eating organic and sustainable foods prepared by the culinary fellow, spending most of my time alone, lonely in the heat of so much luxury, with an orange tube dress stuck to my legs as I walked up and down the long staircase between the upper bedroom and lower studio of the modernist cement cube where I'd been placed. In the side of a hill. I felt so far away from my friends. Unclear as to how I'd arrived in such a place. I took a photo of my face reflected in the computer screen where Todd May's voice came from. Hair piled up in one hand, I have circles under my eyes, I'm taking notes.

In his talk, Todd May talked about friendship. Friendships of tending to, seeking the good of the other for the sake of the other, of some kind of commitment, spontaneous gifts, compliments given when one's friend is feeling vulnerable, doing for one another in the context of shared activities. Being with while ill or dying. *I look and see my friend is equal*, a type of relation without hierarchy, *or at least as little hierarchy as our age allows*. Generally not subject to the economy of credit and debt. He talked about the hidden solidarities of such friendship, its political possibilities, to resist the impoverished subjectivities available under neo-liberalism. He must have meant those who profit by it, neo-liberalism, our relations narrowed to consumer or entrepreneur, near and far sides of production, grounded in the eternal present of buying or the imagined future of investment's return. *Where one speaks even of the overall yield of one's reproductive life.* Where our competition with others does not so much concern what one another of us has made or accomplished, but who has had the best return on their investment.

Friendship, Todd May said, is rooted in the past, *a temporal thickness of shared activities,* my heart swelling a little here, thinking again about all the folding and stapling, rehearsals, setting up chairs and taking them down again. Talking on the phone. Bottles of wine on brick patios. Long histories. Proofreading, getting the next round. Cooking. Trading clothes. Looking in on the cat, feeding the dogs or going on a walk. Being with while ill or dying.

Friendship allows alternative and disruptive communities to form. Shows us another world is possible, already exists. Does away with specific borders. *I look and see my friend is equal. In this sense, irrational.*

Todd May's talk reaches its end at the limits of friendship, which, after all, can only extend to a limited amount of people. Requires time and attention, a level of involvement that precludes a wide circle. There is the inside of friends, and the outside of everyone else. There is the porous border between friendship and enmity. The tendency of one to become another. Some ambivalence, some tension, some feelings that are the opposite of love but also love. Something unstable. A membrane. The limit of a break I kept crashing into.

Such were the conditions in the summer of 2011 that I didn't want to dismiss the importance of friendship, the mostly poets I am and hang out with, even though our interdependencies of work, consumption and residence, our voluntary associations of folding and stapling and fucking, our networks of mutual dependency and support—all still harbored exclusionary and hierarchical relations of private power. Even as we felt, wanted to feel, *otherwise*.

At the anarchist conference in June 2011, Todd May began by saying that he does not want to suggest that having friends, or going out and making more, is necessarily an act of resistance. And yet friendship shows us. Another world is possible. Already exists.

My friends *were* my world in the summer of 2011. What I could see of it. What I couldn't. As the summer before, with difference.

In the summer of 2011, some of my friends were becoming frustrated about and critiquing gender relations among the mostly poets I am and hang out with, and some were organizing around this critique and a general desire to be with other women more often. Others were questioning why a critique of gender relations among the mostly poets I am and hang out with, not exactly a new problem, would vocalize itself just now around the curating practice of a young poet who had recently moved to the area and hosted talks in the bedroom of his apartment where there was only room for a small group of people who either sat on the bunk bed's lower deck or in a circle on the floor. Many were disagreeing with each other and some were finding the resulting conversation useful regardless, including the young poet, who engaged the frustration about his curating practice and remained part of the ongoing conversation. In this way the critique managed to become disentangled from the figure of the young poet and opened onto something larger for a moment, and this process felt somewhat different from other moments I could remember from the shared past of the mostly poets I am and hang out with, from our temporal thickness of shared activities.

Some were walking in the street and on the sidewalk in protest of murders that public transportation private security forces in the Bay Area continued to commit on a regular basis, murders of unarmed men who were often already marginalized because of their race or class or both.

Some were walking and riding their bikes in the street to protest the proposed closure of Oakland library branches.

Some were walking in the street and banging on pots and pans in solidarity with prisoners on hunger strike at Pelican Bay, in protest of inhumane conditions at supermax prisons, the small windowless cells where people are held in indefinite solitary confinement if they are identified as a gang member because of their reading material, or because they said hello to someone previously identified as a gang member.

And still others were organizing anticuts, "a series of counterausterity marches and events, designed to begin assembling an anticapitalist force capable of combating the current age of budget cuts and economic violence." Maybe because I couldn't stop reading about women and resistance movements and had recently read Assata Shakur's autobiography, Diana Block's *Arm the Spirit*, and Susan Stern's *With the Weathermen*, books loaned to me by friends and subsequently suggested to others, I couldn't help but hear, in the name of the group organizing the anticuts, a direct echo of the October 1969 Chicago actions organized by the Weathermen. And couldn't help but think about that moment's many failures, of alliance, of arrogance, of autocratic leadership, the deep problems around gender, the romance of weapons, the covert and illegal attacks by the FBI that splintered and finally destroyed militant social movements in the 1970s. Such were the conditions that, in the summer of 2011, the Weather Underground was a website where one could check the seven-day forecast for cities in the U.S. Often I checked the weather there. As I am trying to narrate this from the future in such a way that takes into account something I cannot see, I wonder how it was I didn't hear, in the name of the group organizing the anticuts, a direct echo of far more recent actions, the "angry Fridays" in Yemen, in Tunisia, in Egypt.

Such were the conditions in the summer of 2011 that I did not want to dismiss the group organizing anticuts, my friends and some friends of the poets I am and hang out with, as they organized a series of counterausterity marches, as they evoked and called forth, Frankenstein style, so many submerged, disjointed histories of resistance, such as the 1946 general strike in Oakland, when huge crowds of people gathered around the triangle of ground where Broadway and Telegraph meet and terminate, the same triangle where this group met to march in the summer of 2011.

I did not want to dismiss the history of the 1946 general strike, in which women workers were a driving force, despite the failure of that strike to meaningfully include African American workers.

I did not want to dismiss the way that this group, friends of the mostly poets I am and hang out with, some who had spent a lot of time organizing and protesting against intense fee hikes in the UC system, were attempting to connect state cuts to public education with proposed cuts to Oakland libraries, and these with the economic violence and prison system that impacts poor young people of color most of all. They were not the only people attempting to do this but they were the ones I could see. My friends, and friends of my friends, were my world. What I could see of it, and what I couldn't.

In the summer of 2011, I attempted to attend the second in a series of counterausterity marches and events designed to begin assembling an anticapitalist force capable of combating the current age of budget cuts and economic violence, organized by some friends of my friends. I didn't know anything. I barely knew them. The march was scheduled for a Friday, mid-afternoon. I discussed the march with two of my friends and we put the date in our respective calendars the same way one might commit to a scary exercise class. I wanted to participate, I was interested, I didn't want to dismiss, I had some curiosity, I was fearful and sweaty, I'd been reading a lot about, but in order to participate I might need to begin participating, full of desire and fear, not unlike my feelings towards a 7.5 scenario on the Hayward Fault, event of which I was most terrified, it took the form of all my other desires, something unexpected on the way. That the earthquake had so obviously already happened—had come and gone in Oakland, in Richmond, in Bayview/Hunters Point, in New Orleans, in Haiti,—did not mean the earthquake was not also still coming. Did not mean the earthquake was not already happening all the time, every day, the magnitude 1.9 or 4.3 or 2.2 tremors I couldn't really feel yet, hadn't seen before, the first nine Food Not Bombs volunteers arrested for sharing meals at the entrance to Golden Gate Park in 1988, or meals shared 24 hours a day in solidarity with the 27-day Tent City protest for homeless peoples rights in San Francisco in 1989, or the covert squatting of 700-800 buildings opened by Homes Not Jails between 1994 and 1999, or the rushing of the Pacific Stock Exchange in Robin Hood outfits in 2001, or City Slicker Farm's backyard gardens program in West Oakland, or the 2003 anti-war pickets that shut down the Port of Oakland, where the Oakland Police Department used concussion grenades, wooden bullets, and beanbags full of metal shot.

A few days before the march my friends and I wobbled—*I'm not sure I can leave work early, I have childcare issues, I definitely can't get out of work before 5, I can't stand marches, is it going to be a march, or something else?* Two of us took the event off our calendars entirely, then two of us put it back on. We'd go together later, after we got off work. We'd meet on the BART platform, ride the train downtown and go find the march at the library, where things were scheduled to wind up.

By the time my friend and I met at BART around 5:30, several arrests had been made, the march reported on briefly by local affiliates. Helicopters circled downtown on the screens and in person. When the group, perhaps 50 of them, perhaps 75, met up at the triangle where Broadway and Telegraph meet and terminate, triangle of ground at the center of the 1946 general strike, many police were waiting. A cop showed one of the marchers a message on his smartphone from police intelligence, a link to the group's website. The group attempted to move one way in the street, the police attempted to move them another. The police were going to arrest someone no matter what. The marchers were going to say FUCK THE PIGS no matter what. A ritual performance, with gestures and counter-gestures, and counter-counter-gestures, a performance to be re-told later, each re-telling another ritual performance. The local news would insist on outside agitators in their re-telling, and the marchers would swagger in theirs.

On the platform, my friend and I made jokes about black hoodies. We didn't really know what to wear to march in the street. In our no longer all that young white female middle class bodies, marching in the street was a form of knowledge and experience we were supposed to have obtained, if at all, during college, or the years between college and a first serious job and/or marriage, knowledge to be slowly abandoned later as professional and domestic duties crowded in, slowly replacing other commitments which we would look back on later with something like nostalgia, or self-satisfaction, or regret, or dismissal, as with anything taken so seriously when young. This is one movie version, one literary novel of what middle age white female middle class bodies can do. Somewhere in mine, a muffled pride at learning late. At the wrong moment. We were not heroic. We didn't know anything. Or we knew the wrong things. We were scared.

I was afraid of not knowing anyone at the march, or not knowing them that well, I carried the usual social anxiety in my body, afraid I would do or say something stupid, afraid it would be obvious I didn't know what I was doing, didn't know what to do with my body, and that in my anxiety I would attempt to pretend as if I did, a habit I had worked for years to break but sometimes still slipped into. If I was nervous and an unfamiliar name came up in conversation, I'd smile and nod my head. It occurred to me this bad habit of anxiety, and the real chance I might say or do something stupid, could have more disastrous results in the street than at a party or reading, could mean more than feeling sweaty and red in the face. I was afraid nobody would have my back, that nobody would have my friend's back, afraid we'd each only have one other's inexperienced backs.

I was afraid too that I might feel comfortable in some way I couldn't predict, might find some friends and friends of my friends at the march and find that I knew my friends better than I realized, afraid that surrounded by friends of my friends on the street, all the anger and distress I felt as I watched the screens all day, as information coursed through me, might cause my body to act unpredictably, spasmodically, putting myself or someone else in danger. I was afraid of getting arrested. Afraid of losing my invisibility with the police and everything that came with that, even though it was a loss my body could afford more than others. Most of the time I was afraid of the police. Most of the time I didn't need to be. I traveled by car. I kept my head down.

Later, while we stood and talked in the hallway at the private women's college where we worked, my friend would remind me, gently more gentle than I could be with myself when in the grips of this fear that was also anger and shame, about fragmentation of the public sphere, dominated by elite interests, which pretty much controlled everything I knew about moving in the street, everything I knew about what to do with my body, and I would remember that most of the time I drove my car, often I checked the weather online, generally I moved between my car and the doorway, between restaurants and bars, the walking path and parking lot, theater and arts space. Mostly I moved between the private and semi-private houses. My body knew how to get money out of an ATM because that's how money had trained it, to shield the keypad with my hand, to be aware of my surroundings without appearing too nervous. My body had been trained to go with the flow, not how to block it.

Later I thought about the house, how the poetry readings, what felt like the most exciting readings, and the friendliest, had increasingly moved into private, into the semi-private house, how the poets I am and hang out with had retreated further and further into semi-private space. We liked very much to party in a semi-private house together and who could blame us, in the impoverishment of our daily relations, subject positions narrowed to that of consumer or entrepreneur, near and far sides of production, grounded in the eternal present of buying or the imagined future of investment's return. I thought about what little information I had about moving together in semi-public with my friends. I had to admit many of my friends had more information about this. Friends who rode to work on their bikes or signed a speaker card at city council meetings or performed in semi-public spaces, performances marked by some degree of physical and social extremity. Friends who had been arrested, or organized a squat. Maybe my lack of information about moving around in semi-public space had nothing to do with a social life built on gathering with others in semi-private houses. Maybe the always gathering in the semi-private house was itself a symptom of something larger, something I couldn't see. There was hardly any public space to be found anymore, anyways. The libraries closing. Everything semi-private, or semi-public.

By the time my friend and I made it downtown on the day we attempted to attend the second in a series of counterausterity marches and events designed to begin assembling an anticapitalist force capable of combating the current age of budget cuts and economic violence, cops lounged on the street in pairs, inasmuch as cops can be said to lounge, they wheeled in tight circles on their bikes. Downtown seemed mostly as ever, halfway abandoned in places, flooded in others with happy hour's arrival, a hazy mid-afternoon light and money piling up softly in it, feathers in bunches, bunched at the seam where buildings meet sidewalk, piles of trash pushed there by the wind, flattened out boxes from McDonald's. Little golden corners. One could almost sit down there.

In the terrible community, one always arrives too late.

I did try to write this book, I did try hard to write it.

I thought California would be different.

Later while I was writing this at the artist residency in the South Bay, eating rich and sustainable foods and walking through the surrounding neighborhoods of empty and enormous houses, houses with small vineyards, the streets empty save for gardeners who tended the lawns and vineyards of empty houses, I met Nancy Popp. This artist who climbs. Light poles and stoplights and signs. Sometimes she goes down into a well by herself for two days, and other times she is covered in honey in the fetal position in a large bowl, but generally she climbs things in semi-public space and hangs out there for a while, long enough to trigger the security guard or administrative staff or Tijuana police. Her legs wrapped around the pole like a koala bear. She hangs out wearing yoga pants and tennis shoes. Sometimes she disappears into the photograph, a piece of the wired skyline, and other times there is a crowd of people peering up. Sometimes a single person, a mall cop, does a double take. Someone is there with a camera to officially document the performance. Many other people are there with cameras coincidentally, because that is what people do in semi-public space in the summer of 2011. The security guard and administrative staff and Tijuana police do not really know what to do with Nancy. Sometimes they hang out with everyone else, peering up. Sometimes they arrest her when she climbs down. Later at the station it all gets cleared up, and she's released: *Oh, it's an art project.* I think a security guard or cop made a joke once about bringing in a cherry picker. This makes me laugh for a second and then I think about bulldozers, the Caterpillar D9T, Jamal Suliman, Rachel Corrie, and feel sick to my stomach. I don't think a security guard or administrative staff person or cop has ever climbed up after her. I think the only person to ever climb up after Nancy was a poet who thought he was *helping*.

When I met Nancy I had this streaming feeling of needing Nancy climbing, streaming needing to feel a body move in semi-public space in any way other than those money taught me. This art practice of climbing light poles or stoplights or signs felt somehow just as important as other art practices such as counterausterity marches. Both triggered the security force, although I wrote this paragraph before a future in which the security force began to show up with a lot more force when triggered, in which the distance between art projects and actions could be measured by the tear gas. A future in which some art projects and actions might overlap completely. Green and yellow messages woven into a chain-link fence with mustard uprooted from the ground, *resistance is fertile*. A future in which a message inscribed with chalk on the street, *art is the weapon,* might trigger a lot of force. Batons to the stomach, non-lethal rounds, arrest.

If ever I wished to summon the narrator from a novel by Roberto Bolaño, it would be now most of all, oh summer of 2011, heading into fall, thickening of a temporal thickness of shared activities and events. The narrator in Roberto Bolaño's novels so often looks back with bemusement on the friendships of youth, groups of poets in Latin America, the high stakes of community, their envy and love and hate, the seriousness with which opinions on literature or politics are argued, opinions they will sometimes change their minds about, or positions they will experience the failure of, moments of recognition arrived at mostly on their own, later, much later, in Europe, in a small apartment, in the lonely present of writing, where so many friends have since disappeared, been disappeared, lost. It's not like the movie or literary novel of what a white middle class female body can do. It's not dismissive, this bemusement, it takes the past seriously as recurrence in the present of writing, looking back with affection and partial knowledge, the present as only ever the past in which one continues in error, the present marked mostly by the loss of a person, who most of the novels spend their time looking for. "Most of us there talked a lot, not just about poetry, but politics, travel (little did we know what our travels would be like,) painting, architecture, photography, revolution and the armed struggle that would usher in a new life and a new era, so we thought, but which, for most of us, was like a dream, or rather the key that would open the door into a world of dreams, the only dreams worth living for. And even though we were vaguely aware that dreams often turn into nightmares, we didn't let that bother us."

For a long time, I had been with my friends, the mostly poets I am and hang out with, at events. We gathered in the auditoriums of art schools and meeting rooms of public universities. We gathered at bookstores and galleries. We gathered in one another's living room to hear one of us, invited by another of us, read poetry, sentences, jokes, translations. Sometimes we sang and told stories. For a long time, I hurried to my car afterwards. After a while I began to stand outside the door of the auditorium and meeting room and bookstore and gallery with my friends, talking. Sometimes we stood on the curb, or walked together to the train or parking lot, talking all the while. After a while I began to walk with my friends to the bar afterwards, or we drove there in our cars, or stood on the porch of the house where someone had just finished reading in the living room. At the bar, on the porch, we stood and talked some more. After a while I began to ride the train with my friends, or we picked one another other up in our cars and used the carpool lane. After a while I began to talk with some of my friends through a receiver pressed to my ear, or through the wire of a headset attached to a smartphone, on which I sent messages to some of my friends by text, which is one way we arranged to meet at bars and restaurants, and sometimes we went to the auditorium or arts space or living room afterwards, and sometimes we just kept drinking and eating together. After a while I met some of my friends more often to go on a walk, or yoga class, an early dinner, a cocktail. After a while I invited some of my friends to my home for dinner, and some of my friends invited me to theirs, and this was different than listening to a reading in the living room. After a while I met my friend's children, or slept on the couch at their house and then woke up and drank coffee together. After a while I told some of my friends my secrets, I called my friends on my smartphone when I felt depressed or panicky. We gossiped and laughed. We discussed our surveillance of one another on the internet. We shared food and clothes and job listings. We spent holidays together and visited each other in the hospital.

If I had not been with my friends in the auditorium and bookstore and art space, how could I have known anything about the way they sit in chairs, or lean forward while listening, how could I know the way their hands hold a pen or move across the pages of a notebook? How could I identify the particular sound of their laughter or sighs? If I had not stood with my friends outside the door talking, how could I know anything about their opinions on literature or politics? And if I had not walked to the train or parking lot with them afterwards, how could I know where they live, or recognize the car they drive? If I had not gone with my friends to the bar, how could I understand the way they tell a joke, or dance, or hold their body when insecure? If I had not spoken with my friends through a receiver pressed to my ear, or a wire connected to the headset of a smart phone, how could I know where to meet up? How could I understand the complicated part about their job? If I had not gone on many walks with my friends, how could I understand the pace of their walking, length of their legs, shape of their thinking? If I had not gone to my friend's home, how could I know of such awkward and tender things, of the bed where they sleep, the single jar of mustard on the refrigerator shelf, the commode into which they shit, their attachment to certain objects, postcards, plants, the place they sit when we talk on the smartphone—how could I picture them there, when we spoke together, or know where to find the supplies, when I came by later to feed the cat or pick up a change of clothes?

How could I know the sound of their voices, if I had not?

In August of 2011, I sat in a group with some of my friends as we convened for a two-day free school. We convened at the public library, the semi-public house, the gallery. In advance of meeting together, we read a book about Bolivia, El Alto, groups of people uprooted from their homes and moved to the city at the same time, groups who arrived together, at once, with shared demands and a lack of private space, with a public square and collective deprivation, collective danger and suffering. Groups of people who knew how to move together to block roads and streets at night, quickly, and to withdraw instantly like a flea bite, simultaneously, at thousands of different locations. Who knew how to form lightning marches and blockades without a route or prior plan, like the flight of the beetle, which seems to lack any predictable direction. How to move like a red ant, and a plumed bird.

I felt some despair as I read this book—how could my friends and I ever learn how to move together, given the uneven distribution of resources and fragmentation of the public sphere? In the sexual division of labor and ordinary daily violence of love, illness, labor, birth, rape, fractured by structural contradictions and imposition of beauty as a condition for social acceptability, divided by legacies of prior organization and political conflict, dominated by elite interests. When so often we acted out, stumbled and tripped, in our feelings that were the opposite of love but also love, when it was so easy to inadvertently intensify a well-known mutual dislike between two others of us, or disrupt our own internal functioning from within, to create suspicion about one another. When our interdependencies of work, consumption, and residence, our voluntary associations of folding and stapling and fucking, our networks of mutual dependency and support all still harbored exclusionary and hierarchical relations of private power.

How could we even learn from this book? What could we know, or do? Stubbornly, I clung to the idea that if I was going to move in the street, I needed to figure it out with my friends. That from a temporal thickness of shared activities, of years spent together folding and stapling, of setting up chairs and taking them down again, talking on the phone, meeting on the platform, being with while ill or dying, that from such long histories of entanglement, even of lying to our girlfriend or boyfriend as we made out in pairs and groups, or publishing mostly white men and then getting defensive when someone pointed it out, we might still find a way to move together like the flea, or beetle, or red ant, or plumed bird.

As we sat in a group at the free school, some of my friends wanted to talk about the special role of poets as language workers. Others were very tired of this idea and maintained poets had no special role as such. Some wanted to talk about the community, the mostly poets I am and hang out, its activation. How to. Some of my friends cried, and said they felt like a hospice worker for a system that is dying. Some spoke of the ocean. Some spoke of action. And then we argued about this, what is and isn't action, how can it be separated from language? Some were impatient with the argument, the group. Some had street cred as activists, and others didn't. We spoke of foreclosure, mutual aid, bananas; spoke of the riots in London, an interview online with two girls who had been up all night drinking rosé. They could not wait to do it again. We spoke of the students running in relays of protest around buildings in Chile. As we spoke, ideas would come to us, and each idea felt like another art project, another failure, even as we opened our mouths to say "I know this sounds crazy but what if we," and when we heard these ideas leave our mouths and hover for a moment, we quickly turned them into jokes instead. Little failed art projects. *Jogging and rosé.*

One of us talked about how tired he was of the idea one could only work with one's friends. Someone else talked about working with people who one dislikes or is irritated by. And another talked about the incredible feeling of being on the street with many people, strangers, who are suddenly one's friends, friends because of suddenly moving.

I said, *it's like zero to riot.*

The day after the free school ended, I rode in a car across the bridge with some friends. We met up with more friends and together descended into the Civic Center BART station to protest the murders that public transportation private security forces in the Bay Area continued to commit on a regular basis, murders of unarmed men already marginalized by race or class or both. Descended to protest BART's shut-off of subterranean cell phone service in its downtown San Francisco stations the week earlier, a shut-off intended to prevent a similar protest. On the platform, more reporters than protesters. More cops than reporters. We circled like a drain. One friend zig zagged across the platform with a phone in his hand, singing over and over *can you hear me now*? It was a crazy idea one of us might have spoken and turned into a joke but this friend sang the joke instead. Some sang along with the joke in high-pitched voices. Others sang along in low-pitched voices. Others sang while standing directly in front of a cop, leaning in, bellowing *can you hear me now*? Some of my friends sat on the ground and wrote on red paper hearts with markers. BART STOP KILLING US NOW. Sitting helped one of my friends calm down but I couldn't sit, couldn't calm down. I hadn't intended to descend, somehow thought I could stay above ground, maybe at the fare gates, maybe thought the station would be closed when we arrived. Instead I got my ticket and rode down thinking am I really going to protest in the primal scene of my panic attacks? I careened around the platform as commuters trickled out. Soon the trains didn't stop at the platform, just rushed through the station on schedule, while riot cops so many more of them than us started lining up at either end of the platform in front of the escalators, while my friend careened, singing his beautiful and comic song, while my friends sat on the ground and wrote messages, taped their hearts to the wall, and my body propelled itself through the line and up the escalator, full of shame and unable to breathe, and had the first dispersal order even been given? *I have to go I have to go* I said something like that what was I anyways a bundle of something wet and oozing, something from the past or future, someone on whom, in her childhood, the rod had not been spared, and my friends calmly saying *ok sweetie we're just going to stay here for a little while longer* and my heart exploding I couldn't breathe careened across Market to the buses, lined up and waiting to take my friends away. When they rose up on escalators moments later like angels in a rush of relief I saw them, not at all in handcuffs. We milled around for a while on the street. Instantly bored and a little disappointed. The cops had cleared the station so quickly after all. More reporters than protesters, more cops than protesters. Some people walked to the Mission and some of us drove home.

A few weeks later, the summer nearly over, a friend asked me to write something for the 2011 Labor Day gathering, WORKING*WRITING*FIGHTING. Had it only been a year?

I wrote something for the Labor Day gathering about Sheila de Bretteville crying about money in Lynn Hershman Leeson's documentary film *!Women Art Revolution*. Crying about the feminist art movement's focus on women's exclusion from systems of power, rather than identification with others who also lacked money and power.

That moment when several of us started crying about student loan debt at the Department retreat.

The swagger of one art project's dismissal of other art projects.

The dismissal of care, or something about splitting material from emotional care.

Something about Etel Adnan's *To Be In A Time Of War*.

To be the panic of constant information.

To somewhat falsely oppose decomposition and insurrection.

To be intimidated by the debt collector. To seek assistance from a non-profit.

To be ashamed of one's self.

To be full of desire and fear.

To be making art projects. To be making art projects together.

"Every miscarriage is a work accident."

To be Claire Fontaine, to be dismissive of Claire Fontaine, to find Claire Fontaine somehow useful. To pivot and grind. To frottage with Claire Fontaine.

"The return of the repressed threatens all my projects of work, research, politics. Does it threaten them or is it the truly political thing in myself, to which I should give relief and room? (…) The silence failed this part of myself that desired to make politics, but it affirmed something new. There has been a change, I have started to speak out, but during these days I have felt that the affirmative part of myself was occupying all the space again. I convinced myself of the fact that the mute woman is the most fertile objection to our politics. The non-political digs tunnels that we mustn't fill with earth."

I don't know why I ended there, with that quotation, in the thing I wrote for the Labor Day gathering, as the summer of 2011 rushed towards fall. I keep saying *I don't know*. It seems important. When so many around me claim to. So many books diagnose the conditions. So many posts claim what is to be done. With a trail of comments to argue the finer points. While the conditions keep repeating. Proliferate. Where so little changes, I don't know, it seems important. To "stay with it." Not knowing.

And yet the pages feel rigid. I keep seizing up around everything I still can't see. Seizing up around the wounded part. I took something personally, something ripping or tearing in the body, in the family, in the home sort of, in the guts. When I pull my hand away from the bandage and look down, the opening is very small. Healed over. Run my hand across the rash. A mountain that gave birth to a mouse. A song and dance about nothing. A struggle against part of myself. The low body with a new voice full of desire and fear. *I look and see my friend is equal.* A type of strike that involves the whole life. *We need to change ourselves.* I wanted nothing short of the movement that could potentially contaminate anyone. My body full of you, we struggled against ourselves together. I don't know. The sound nobody recognized. Over and over again. His ragged breath those last few hours, the sponge at his mouth. *The Community of Those Who Have Nothing In Common.* Arms pinned behind his back, held down on the platform. Surrounded on the pavement, blood leaking out. I didn't know how to write about it. I didn't know. I was in common. With those who have nothing in common.

THE WIND BLOWS

You don't need a title to be a leader. You don't need a new idea to start a business. You don't need a boyfriend to feel good. You don't need a mythical club membership to call Yahoo's patent threat against Facebook desperate. You don't need a helicopter to travel like the bachelor. You don't need a DSLR camera to take good pictures, a computer to make a poster, a huge list to sell your Ebook. You don't need a cyber attack to take down the North American Power Grid, and you don't need David Harvey to know what time it is: small-batch production and social movements. Idiolect and anarchy. Charismatic politics and rhetoric. Temporary contracts and electronic reproduction. Fictitious capital and localism. And he published that book, *The Condition of Postmodernity*, in 1991. What's real time?

"In the twinkling of an eye" "all that is solid dissolves into air" "shattered glass and toppling masonry"

Retarded time: in which "the future becomes present so late as to be outmoded as soon as it is crystallized." That's from a 1964 graph by someone named Gurvitch, who associates social formations with particular senses of time. Harvey says academics and other professionals seem perpetually condemned to this retarded time. I laughed when I read this. Retarded time is associated with feudalism, guilds, community and its social symbols. The professionalization of poetry. Produced in small batches. Print on demand.

Table 3.2 Gurvich's typology of social times

Type	Level	Form	Social formations
Enduring time	ecological	continuous time in which past is projected in the present and future; easily quantifiable	kinships and locality groupings (particularly rural peasant societies and patriarchal structures)
Deceptive time	organized society	long and slowed down duration masking sudden and unexpected crises and ruptures between past and present	large cities and political 'publics'; charismatic and theocratic societies
Erratic time	social roles, collective attitudes (fashion) and technical mixes	time of uncertainty and accentuated contingency in which present prevails over past and future	non-political 'publics' (social movements and fashion-followers); classes in process of formation
Cyclical time	mystical unions	past, present and future projected into each other accentuating continuity within change; diminution of contingency	astrology-followers; archaic societies in which mythological, mystical and magical beliefs prevail
Retarded time	social symbols	future becomes present so late as to be outmoded as soon as it is crystallized	community and its social symbols; guilds, professions etc. feudalism

The time of this book is definitely retarded. I started writing it in January 2011. It ends on September 8th of the same year with a protest at the BART Powell Street station, one in a series of relentless public demonstrations in protest of BART police murder of Charles Hill. During the first of these in August, BART turned off cell phone service at several stations. Anonymous called for a protest of that decision which is when things started to snowball, protests of BART police murders past and present but also in defense of free speech and the right to assemble. So it came to be that you might see Krystof from NO JUSTICE NO BART standing next to someone in a Guy Fawkes mask. It was kind of weird and great. People seemed slightly anxious, a little skeptical about this convergence, despite Anonymous operations earlier in the year supporting movements in Tunisia and Egypt. Anonymous seemed so wacky and chaotic. What was their deal. Were they all sociopathic dude geeks. What did you think about that leak of BART employee home addresses? Seriously, what's up with the Guy Fawkes thing.

Monday after Monday in August and September the protests continued, *no justice, no peace, disband the BART police*, sometimes protesters jogged through stations and around and around downtown, the SFPD running after them, and other times police kettled people in the station and arrested them in large groups, which is what happened on September 8. I watched it on the internet, my friends in the kettle, I saw Ted and others milling around. Also in the kettle: an entire class of journalism students from SF State. Which is where this book ends.

Yet here it is 2012 I'm still writing it. There's a word this book won't say, a future it refuses to name because it's too soon to know anything about it. Lil Wayne says "I don't need a watch, the time is now or never," and that's the way this future feels, its presence washes back through everything I've written, rendering the book outmoded even as it crystallizes. Something changed in the fall of 2011, something happened, almost immediately after the BART protests I kept thinking of as another failure. Which is partly why I ended this book there, with a protest I watched on the internet because when I went IRL earlier in the month I had a panic attack on the platform. As I toggled between twitter and facebook on September 8 there seemed to be, as ever, more reporters than protesters, more cops than reporters. On the local news, commuters spoke overwhelmingly of their annoyance, this disruption of travel home from work.

Glen Park BART attacked: We didn't do it for the lulz. That's what Some Bay Area Anarchists posted on IndyBay the morning of September 9th, claiming responsibility for smashed fare machines and turnstiles the night before, at a station many stops past Powell. *Our spray cans dispensed slogans and our hammers shattered screens and ticket readers.* This happened about the same time some of my friends and some people I didn't know and an entire class of journalism students from SF State were milling around in the kettle. *We look to each other to find meaning and reject the limiting discourse of rights and free speech as a vehicle for our rage.* After taking some shots at Anonymous, after rejecting the structure of demand, after predicting some possible responses, like condemnation on the grounds that violence against property promotes state repression, Some Bay Area Anarchists signed off: *Freedom to those arrested at today's Powell Street action. See you at the barricades.*

Probably a lot could be said from the future about September 8 and diversity of tactics, and endless arguments about diversity of tactics. About the uneasy convergence of hammers and lulz, nurses and the homeless, longshoreman and pre-school teachers, veterans and college students, librarians and the unemployed, poets and academics. A lot could be said about Saturday nights, and FTP marches to come: *All police are the enemy. We articulate this when we choose to honor the lives of Oscar Grant, Charles Hill and Kenneth Harding by fighting for our own lives.*

So many of the names I saw Twitter showed up later in a future this book can't name, in which anyone might show up, and many often did. I found them so beautiful the names I didn't know. Tiqqun says "The end of the terrible community coincides with an opening to events: around these events, the singularities group, learn to cooperate and reach out to one another." I have been thinking for a long time for years I have not been able to stop thinking about something John Ashbery writes, "I thought that if I could put it all down, that would be one way. And next the thought came to me that to leave all out would be another, and truer, way."

Whenever I tried to put it all down (poetry community, my friends) I left all out (Oakland, Oscar Grant.) Whenever I left all out (betrayal, grief) I put it all down (earthquakes, conferences.) The beautiful names, the singularities somehow felt like putting it all down and leaving all out at the same time. In the same space.

Something thrashes, seeks its escape, flops and tries to slide past, to the side of, under, or through the isolation of the terrible community. Its incapacity to get beyond itself, its agitated inertia, its worn relationships, its diffuse self-surveillance.

Something thrashes, seeks its escape, flops and tries to slide past, to the side of, under or through the isolation of the terrible writing project, the thing I made that failed. How could it have been otherwise? What could ever be adequate to the death of a man I didn't know, his body marked by race, class, location. Shot in the back by the hand of a private police force, the hand of crowd control.

Many things did not change in the fall of 2011. For everything that happened in the future something else happened, something that had been happening for a long time. It kept on happening. In New Orleans. In East New York, Brooklyn. In Little Rock. In Monterey

Park. In Cypress Hills, Brooklyn. In Bushwick, Brooklyn. In Calumet City. In Bronx. In San Clemente. In Dotham. In Sanford. In Galveston. In New Orleans. In Dayton. In Kershaw County. In West Bend. In Gainesville. In New Orleans. In Newburgh. In Wichita. In Aurora. In Maple Heights, Cleveland. In Pasadena. In Atlanta. In San Leandro. In Baltimore. In Atlanta. In Chicago.

It happened when he led them on a chase. When he called for assistance. When the SWAT Unit was serving a drug-related search warrant. When they tased him in the face and he didn't surrender. When they thought he was involved in a carjacking. When he allegedly attempted a mugging. When he had a small pen knife. When he was a child with Asperger's Syndrome. After they chased him into his home. While his daughters waited for him in the car. When they assumed he was a threat to the girls. When he was intoxicated. When he looked suspicious. When they suspected he was under the influence of drugs. When they thought he looked suspicious. When he was attempting to keep an appointment to babysit his children. When he tried to avoid a drug traffic stop. When he ran away and hid on a neighbor's back porch after the police broke up a party. When he behaved "strangely." When he was shirtless and wearing pajama bottoms. When the house was raided for marijuana. When he allegedly came at four of them with a knife. When he allegedly refused the order to drop a gun. When he allegedly jumped on the hood of a squad car. When he was speeding. When he was falsely accused of stealing a laptop. When he was trying to protect his sister. When he was in custody. When his mother said her son only had a small pocket knife. When he was a teenager and attended high school.

What could I ever write.

And while many of the poets I am and hang out with might have previously understood the explicit connections between something that had been happening for a long time and uneven distribution of resources, maybe some of us understood these connections intellectually before the fall of 2011.

At some point we began to feel it in our ribs, and all along the face.

Gertrude Stein says "I write for myself and strangers," which I found sort of terrible when I first heard it as a young person. I may have said to myself that sounds elitist. Austere, and lonely. Probably because I write for myself and my friends. Obviously this is a real limitation. It is almost impossible to write for your friends and strangers at the same time.

Perhaps it is becoming clear, dear reader, it is unlikely this book will end with me masking up and joining friends and strangers in the street. Although in a future in which anyone might show up I did too, even if I put it all down, what a sad and small collection it would make. A figure in impractically high-heeled black oxfords running from her car to the camp, arms full of photocopies made at work. A figure hunched over a laptop, stomach churning, donating to the bail fund on paypal. She stands in the crowd and looks around anxiously while scrolling the feed on her smartphone. Brings leftover trays of sushi to the GA, boxes of cupcakes originally donated to the theater where Clive works. A figure who stubbornly continues to show up only to leave shortly after she arrives. I couldn't stay but neither could I stay away. In a future in which anyone might show up, a figure watches the livestream and loves her friends. The poets are ecstatic but also matter of fact. Some move further in and lock arms when the call comes. Some take photographs. Make signs. Bring the speakers. Off and on, they are really, really scared. Tired. Annoyed, skeptical, aggressive. Post-camp messianic.

In a future in which anyone might show up, as some of my friends began to move further in, their identity as poets slowly slipped away.

My friend said another friend says it's hard to hang onto being a poet at a certain point you're just an anarchist. As the singularities group.

As some of my friends stayed on the edge, their identity as poets became if anything somewhat more pronounced.

Around the edges of a plaza that is also the wide open internet, as some of my friends moved further in and others stayed on the edge, skirmishes broke out. Who was and wasn't there, in what capacity. Why or why not. Skirmishes about action and tactics and also aesthetics. Still skirmishing the role of poetry in such a future. Everybody moving further in wanted everybody else to move further in too, probably because it is better that way, more pleasure, and safety. More can happen.

Some of the mostly poets I am and hang out with felt invigorated as they moved further in. Some I think felt strong, and brave. Some felt manic, anxious, sweaty. Some were relieved to take a break from the non-stop sociality of the mostly poets I am and hang out with, the readings where one might often see the same people, might feel somewhat bored, or tired of talking about insurrectionary texts, tired of cringing and wincing, or frustrated with the project that published work by mostly white men, might feel pushed out of the milieu's circumference, that porous border between friendship and enmity, the tendency of one to become another. And some moved fluidly, with pleasure between the non-stop sociality of the mostly poets and non-stop action of the plaza, some felt joy in this movement, and appreciated the way poetry entered the plaza, it felt important poetry have a place there, but others felt annoyed when readings were scheduled during an all day workshop on contemporary uprisings, U.S. labor history, and worker cooperatives. Some made new friends or lovers as they moved further in. Some felt surprised at their willingness to continue to be in the presence of a militarized police force over and over again, despite the sweatiness and anxiety, despite the confusion.

Everybody who didn't or couldn't move further in—I'm not sure. I am that figure, sort of. I want to say they feel vulnerable. Dependent on chance or circumstance, uncertain, liable to fail, exposed to risk, insecure, unstable, but what do I know. Some I think felt defensive. Some were over-employed or over-committed. Over-medicated or under-medicated. Skeptical or exhausted. Hopeless or tender. Having a panic attack. Some did their best to support those who moved further in, to support from the edge.

Everybody I think felt confused. Everybody who moved further in, everybody who didn't or couldn't—everybody feels vulnerable I think. Whether at the edge, or further in. Off and on heroic. Everybody dependent on chance or circumstance, uncertain, liable to fail, exposed to risk, insecure, unstable. But with difference. With more or less padding. The bruised and detained bodies of those who moved further in. The plea bargains and stay away orders that brought them into closer circulation with families and neighborhoods destabilized by the violent policing of gang injunctions.

And yet under it all, without ceasing, skirmishes about action and tactics and aesthetics. Still skirmishing the role of poetry in such a future. Still hampered by exclusionary and hierarchical relations of private power harbored within our voluntary associations and networks of mutual dependency and support. Still creating suspicion about one another. The minor disputes that so often blocked our communication, blocked the circulation between those who were willing to be in the presence of a militarized police force and those who weren't. Those who couldn't. Who showed up where and who didn't and how did it show up in the writing later. Mostly the writing was heroic. Not showing up mostly didn't show up. In the writing.

Sometimes the heroine of a 19th century novel in my mind will whip her horse in tearful frustration when the animal refuses and goes down on its knees. Or maybe I am thinking of Kirsten Dunst in *Melancholia*, who does exactly that at the edge of a bridge neither she nor her horse can cross. She raises her eyes to the star that is a planet getting closer, the destruction that is coming, the star that is a planet that will obliterate the bubble she lives in with her sister, her family. A bubble of anxiety and depression and property and wealth. Charlotte Gainsbourg whimpers and looks away as the star that is a planet arrives. Kirsten Dunst is calm. The light is yellow. They hold hands. Charlotte Gainsbourg whimpers and shakes right up to the end. Through the deafening skid of arrival.

In a future in which anyone might show up, bubbles are bursting everywhere, with a gurgling sound, full to the point of breaking open, lacking stability, arriving suddenly, coming apart or seeming to come apart with sudden utterance or expression. As they do the mostly poets I am and hang out with find ourselves either without or aware in a new way of the protective envelopes we've been living in, the transparent glass or plastic domes, the protective but also isolating cover of employment, skin color, class background, house, apartment, bank account. Our identity as poets.

Everybody feels dependent on chance or circumstance, uncertain, liable to fail, exposed to risk, insecure, unstable. But with difference. With more or less padding.

When one of my friends read this she thought I should try to forgive myself. She asked if there was a way to walk forward. So I tried to do something and failed. How could it be otherwise? What could I ever write. Maybe a figure learns, maybe in writing, in paragraphs, inadequacy. Maybe a figure doesn't. There is a dead body here. Several. Oscar Grant, my father. They are particular, marked differently. Their conditions, as in life, asymmetrical. I cannot properly attend to either body, either death, nor to the asymmetry of conditions. It's almost impossible to move. I can't write about it, and I can't not. *If I always feel insufficient or inadequate, what would sufficiency, or what would adequacy be?*

I keep noting the time in this book. And yet I cannot untangle it. The more I notice the more tangled it gets. Is it really now or never—explosive time? Or deceptive time? Time in advance of itself (rushing forward)?

Individual spaces and times in social life   225

Table 3.2 cont.

Type	Level	Form	Social formations
Alternating time	rules, signals, signs and collective conduct	past and future compete in the present; discontinuity without contingency	dynamic economic groups; transition epochs (inception of capitalism)
Time in advance of itself (rushing forward)	collective transformative action and innovation	discontinuity, contingency; qualitative change triumphant; the future becomes present	competitive capitalism; speculation
Explosive time	revolutionary ferment and collective creation	present and past dissolved into a transcendent future	revolutions and radical transformations of global structures

What happened in September of 2011, in October and November, the future this book can't name happened also in the past, from and for it. Time moved forwards and backwards. For every moment in the future in which I was unable there were others. They were small. But they happened. Raking leaves and dirt with five strangers in a parking lot next to the Gill Tract, a 13-acre piece of land administered by UC Berkeley, reclaimed in the future for three weeks. Where hundreds of people came together to plow, prep, and plant over 70 two hundred-foot rows of crops. We raked together in silence. Unlatched from the clock light went on and on, I got sweaty and took off my coat. Such moments returned me to and even sort of soothed the inflamed part, who loves to stack chairs and fold and staple little books, the part that still felt so hurt, the part who had a rash. Returned me to the theater collective, all the actors and directors and teachers who moved Clive and me from house to house in 2001 or was it 2002, they showed up early in the big yellow truck and helped sweep the kitchen after. They moved as one body, the group that looked like a collective but wasn't really, the never-really-a-collective from whom Clive was later so estranged, so hurt, so disbelieving people could ever get together. Both of us still so inflamed. So disbelieving.

And so I called out to the singularities, the names I didn't know, called them out in rooms full of poets. Called out the names I didn't know to the names I did. Maybe it looks like a retreat to poetry. But really it was all I had. The names. The calling. Yosefa Raz's MANIFESTO ON WEAKNESS, Samantha Giles' HURDIS ADDO, Claire Fontaine's HUMAN STRIKE WITHIN THE LIBIDINAL FIELD OF THE ECONOMY, Simone Forti's HANDBOOK IN MOTION, Debbie Hu's TO HEARTBREAK HOTEL.

I called out even though for some part of me, the animal that refuses and goes down on its knees, so hurt, so disbelieving, time stood still. The part on whom the rod had not been spared. In the future I could not stop typing that phrase, "on whom the rod had not been spared," could not stop thinking about physical discipline I received as a child, its apparently limitless imprint, something in my body of which I remained mostly unaware until I tried to stand and this part couldn't, the same part that had a job, the discipline of wages, of institutions, of communities, the compression of space and time, a body thrashing and flopping, for some part of me the clock stands stuck at never although that is clearly wrong, the time is clearly now. And so I continued to love and fear the earthquake most of all, or one version of that metaphor. Under the borders, the fault. Its interruptive power. It is always happening and happening and then something happens and it fails. That is when it happens, the earthquake always happens now. It can be never for a very, very long time. And then it can be now.

Somewhere in the middle of the thing I made that failed Oscar Grant, Raheim Brown.

Somewhere in the middle of the thing I made that failed Raheim Brown, Charles Hill.

Somewhere in the middle of the thing I made that failed Charles Hill, Kenneth Harding.

Somewhere in the middle of the thing I made that failed Kenneth Harding, *Elizabeth Zoë Lindsay Drink Fanta* by Jon Leon.

Somewhere in the middle of the thing I made that failed Charles Hill, *a/s/l* by Uyen Hua.

Somewhere in the middle of the thing I made that failed Raheim Brown, *Occasional Work and Seven Walks from the Office for Soft Architecture* by Lisa Robertson.

Shot five times, twice in the face, somewhere in the middle of *Occasional Work and Seven Walks from the Office for Soft Architecture* by Lisa Robertson.

Shot three times on the platform somewhere in the middle of *a/s/l* by Uyen Ha.

Shot five times in the back somewhere in the middle of *Elizabeth Zoë Lindsay Drink Fanta* by Jon Leon.

Somewhere in the middle of *Elizabeth Zoë Lindsay Drink Fanta* by Jon Leon, Kenneth Harding was riding a Muni train when SFPD officers detained him in the middle of *The Iovis Trilogy: Colors in the Mechanism of Concealment* by Anne Waldman for not having proof of paying the $2 fare in the middle of *The Trees The Trees* by Heather Christle he ran somewhere in the middle of *I Am a Very Productive Entrepeneur* by Mathias Svalina WARNING: VERY GRAPHIC he is lying on the pavement in the middle of *Conversation* by Stephen Ratcliffe, blood pouring out of his body as he makes feeble attempts to move somewhere in the middle of *She, A Blueprint* by Michelle Naka Pierce and Sue Hammond West police officers train their guns on him and create a barrier to hold back an increasingly upset crowd in the middle of *Snow Sensitive Skin* by Taylor Brady and Rob Halpern

SFPD Chief Greg Suhr admitted that police officers killed Harding but said it was justified because Harding shot first but all eye-witnesses said Harding was unarmed in the middle of

The Spiritual Life of Replicants by Murat Nemet-Nejat the SFPD came out with more press releases in the middle of *Status* by Marvin K. White with supposedly conclusive evidence including gun residue on Harding's right hand and a .380 caliber round found in his pocket but somewhere in the middle *Universal Beach* by Vivek Narayanan the gun residue has not been confirmed by an independent party.

Then the SFPD completely changed their story and claimed Harding shot himself in the neck while running from them.

Somewhere in the middle of *The Persians by Aeschylus* by Brandon Brown, somewhere in the middle of the thing I made that failed Oscar Grant, Callie

Callie_hoo Callie somewhere in the middle of *Birds of Tifft* by Jonathan Skinner the march began at Dolores Park where nearly 200 departed and began moving towards the Castro, Anonymous

OperationLeakS Anonymous somewhere in the middle of *My Rice Tastes Like the Lake* by Tsering Wangmo Dhompa the crowd was big enough to block both sides of Market, Jembit Nash

JemWing Jembit Nash somewhere in the middle of *Shoo-Ins to Ruin* by Evan Kennedy blocking tracks, breaking the windows on trains and busses, attacking agents, fighting with the police, East Bay Citizen

eastbaycitizen East Bay Citizen
Chucky

Sonny0utlaw Sonny 0utlaw
AnonNcarolina

an0nyc Anonyorkcity
Anonyorkcity

AnonNCarolina AnonNcarolina
Sonny 0utlaw

idrobinhood Chucky
Eden DaSilva

chanchanz chanchan
Dylan

tomprete Tom Prete
a.dare

astriddare a.dare
Tom Prete

SustainablDylan Dylan
chanchan

edendasilva Eden DaSilva
wholegrain

ip2k Hello There
DeepSouth Anon Medic

tigerbeat Steve Rhodes
Vince in the Bay

VinceintheBay Vince in the Bay
Hello There

Steve Rhodes
AnonMedicDS DeepSouth Anon Medic

wggoodness wholegrain
PrisonReformMovement

bradleycannons Brad Wilson
Uncle Fishbits

RGreenberg R Greenberg
Ck

moui ♥ Moui ♥
Natalia Vasquez

BrknSdwlkFrm Broken Sidewalk Farm
Josh Wolf

Parallax9 Parallax Nine
Parallax Nine

joshwolf Josh Wolf
Broken Sidewalk Farm

NataliaVaskez Natalia Vasquez
♥ Moui ♥

Cksmoka Ck
R Greenberg

UncleFishbits Uncle Fishbits
Brad Wilson

PrisonReformMvt PrisonReformMovement
Cassie Becker

Not2Fear Me[L]
JÆNøÆŃŸMØuŞ

hannejalborg Hanne Jalborg
Samantha

jasonlegate Jason Legate
Elissa Torres

KatherineNGrant Katherine Grant
The Shadow

luvbrrdz LuvBrrdz
LuvBrrdz

TheShadowSF The Shadow
Katherine Grant

elissaANNtorres Elissa Torres
Jason Legate

PrettyAnonymiss Samantha
Hanne Jalborg

MammutGoat511 JÆNøÆŃŸMØuŞ
Me[L]

trivia_tidbit Cassie Becker
Anonymous Watcher

CrappyTires CrappyTires
Emily

AnonymousAgent1 Anonymous
Dustin M. Slaughter

keepheaux You With The Head
David&GoliathProject

LulzTurtle LulzTurtle
\m/ Mody

VivianHo Vivian Ho
Lindseysaid

xcang Charlene Ng
⊕melissa⊕

ItsTechLeech Tech Leech Official
Eric Lahti

ERICLAHTAYYY Eric Lahti
Tech Leech Official

forever_flavor6 ⊕melissa⊕
Charlene Ng

Lindseysaid Lindseysaid
Vivian Ho

SlipknotMody \m/ Mody
LulzTurtle

DavGolProject David&GoliathProject
You With The Head

DustinSlaughter Dustin M. Slaughter
Anonymous

anonimaem Emily
CrappyTires

der_bluthund Anonymous Watcher
Patrick Connors

girljournalist Staci Baird
Steve Streza

lpandell Lexi Pandell
Project Mayhem+

JackalAnon Jackal
Jay E

YourAnonNews Anonymous
Anonymous

frogetteca Nathan S
Solidarity Wisconsin

miriam_schultz Miriam
jane jane

kangaroosexy kangaroo sexy
Darren Embry

dsevil Darren Embry
kangaroo sexy

janesherd jane jane
Miriam

WIProud Solidarity Wisconsin
Nathan S

Anonymously37 Anonymous
Anonymous

jazzidiot Jay E
Jackal

Wotansson Project Mayhem+
Lexi Pandell

SteveStreza Steve Streza
Staci Baird

uppityfag Patrick Connors
Red Workerbot

SkyeX Skye X
Extended Learning

EisMC2 Emmi Einstein
Just A Nobody

Douglaslucas Douglas Lucas
SF Examiner

AnonPlus Anon Plus
apeman homosapien

Anonymous_Edu Anonymous Edu
Op BART

_URGE URGE
OpCOPS

SexyFawkes Sexy Fawkes
Sexy Fawkes

OpCOPS OpCOPS
URGE

OpBART Op BART
Anonymous Edu

apeman_sapien apeman homosapien
Anon Plus

sfexaminer SF Examiner
Douglas Lucas

sirrogue2 Just A Nobody
Emmi Einstein

SFStateExtended Extended Learning
Skye X

RedWorkerbot Red Workerbot
No One

TexasCommie Brandon Ivey
Unkown Nobody

MindDetonat0r Over 9000.
Over 9000.

partygnome Unkown Nobody
Brandon Ivey

mermaidsrcsluts No One
Lucy Berry

xDoom900x Dunno
Evan EStrange Perry

VivaAnonymous Anonymous
insidebayarea

AnonymousNute Nute Nobody
Joanne Michele

mku77 mku77
Renaud Lavoie

SFWeekly SF Weekly
SF Weekly

Ren97RBLX Renaud Lavoie
mku77

SabzBrach Joanne Michele
Nute Nobody

insidebayarea insidebayarea
Anonymous

EStrangeNoise Evan EStrange Perry
Dunno

lsberry1 Lucy Berry
Lead by Example

SoufiandMe Soufi & Me
emilie

AaronBrees AaronBrees
thndur1

MasafumiNegishi Masafumi Negishi
Jessica Goss

timeoutcorner Andrew McInnes
marco iacoboni

marcoiacoboni marco iacoboni
Andrew McInnes

news_snooze Jessica Goss
Masafumi Negishi

thndur1 thndur1
AaronBrees

emilie_manning emilie
Soufi & Me

Anti_Secret Lead by Example
reclaim UC

Der_Maverick Ahmed Medien
Audrey Cooper

UnifiedLeft Unified Left
K

_ANONomatopoeia Anonymous
Anonymous

Korgasm_ K
Unified Left

audreycoopersf Audrey Cooper
Ahmed Medien

reclaimuc reclaim UC
WikiLeaksLover

NOH8ER WikiLeaksLover
Alisha B.

melbeeza Mel
min reyes

stfudvs stfudvs
crixusrising

quester09 Barbara AnneArchy
Asher Wolf

Asher_Wolf Asher Wolf
Barbara AnneArchy

crixusrising crixusrising
stfudvs

Min_Reyes min reyes
Mel

AKBeliever Alisha B.
armanino

veilleange Kelly Goff
Rachaelove

soundwave1234 Roy Morris
puppy

AnonNewsINT AnonNewsINT
AnonNewsINT

_4Puppy a puppy
Roy Morris

CherryDarliiing Rachaelove
Kelly Goff

armaninodaycare armanino
Will Kane

jude @Jude
Felipe de la Rosa

Fdelarosa59 Felipe de la Rosa
@Jude

WgKane Will Kane
☆☆Jazzie Que™☆☆

Donna_Chan Donna Chan
Bliss Kaine

Tigressreow Tigress Lyn Reow
Breaking News

swellyn sue hepner
oink!

ithunk rax
rax

oinktheporkco oink!
sue hepner

___BreakingNews Breaking News
Tigress Lyn Reow

BlissKaine Bliss Kaine
Donna Chan

JazzieBeautiful ☆☆Jazzie Que™☆☆
justin berton

Unid3adX Lulzsec
Sandy Lopez

Celo399 Marcelo Vilela
Brenden

Ghostpickles poems
Christine

Santana_Diavolo Santana Diavolo
Argyle Sabrina

alexhundert alex hundert
Siddhartha Gautama

captblacksheep Siddhartha Gautama
alex hundert

ArgyleSabrina Argyle Sabrina
Santana Diavolo

ChrstineCre8s Christine
poems

brenden Brenden
Marcelo Vilela

JournalismSandy Sandy Lopez
Lulzsec

justinberton justin berton
Under the Dome

sflawdisorder SF Law & Disorder
BART Diaries

munidiaries Muni Diaries
Muni Diaries

bartdiaries BART Diaries
SF Law & Disorder

sfunderthedome Under the Dome
callie

OfficialRabbits 7WhiteRabbits ✔
no justice no bart

pixplz Justin Beck
no justice no bart

roaming_radical Nikolas Koehler
Lisa Carmack

britbarsotti Brittney Barsotti
Liz Tozlian Ireland

nozomimagine nozomi hayase
Jessica Schimm

SpencerTDeVine Spencer Devine
Kristin Hanes

DanHillReports Dan Hill
Elijah Nouvelage

jeffniblack jeffniblack
jeffniblack

Wawanderinghome Elijah Nouvelage
Dan Hill

KristinHanes Kristin Hanes
Spencer Devine

JessicaSchimm Jessica Schimm
nozomi hayase

CappThisGirl Liz Tozlian Ireland
Brittney Barsotti

lisacarmack Lisa Carmack
Nikolas Koehler

nojusticenobart no justice no bart
Justin Beck

nojusticenobart no justice no bart
7WhiteRabbits ✔

callie

callie_hoo callie

(September 8, 2011)